HEARTS OF SENIORS

HEARTS OF SENIORS

A Celebration of Life

Loretta Martin and Susan Massoud

iUniverse, Inc.

New York Lincoln Shanghai

Hearts of Seniors
A Celebration of Life

iUniverse books may be ordered through booksellers or by contacting:

iUniverse
2021 Pine Lake Road, Suite 100
Lincoln, NE 68512
www.iuniverse.com
1-800-Authors (1-800-288-4677)

The views expressed in this work are solely those of the author and do not necessarily reflect the views of the publisher, and the publisher hereby disclaims any responsibility for them.

ISBN: 978-0-595-41581-6 (pbk)
ISBN: 978-0-595-85929-0 (ebk)

Printed in the United States of America

We dedicate this book to our loving and supportive families
and to all the seniors who have passed on since our interviews

CONTENTS

Acknowledgments

Our heartfelt thanks,
to all the extraordinary seniors
who have enriched our lives
by sharing their thoughts and feelings
throughout the many hours of interviews.
We acknowledge Padraic Martin,
Margie Powell, Shirley Hendricksen,
Sandy Ratliff, Becca Martin,
Tyrus Fouchey, and the Old Country Buffet,
for their photographic contributions.
Thanks to Shuling Wu, Dawn Schultz, Kim Hoskin-Sinko, Mike Cui,
Michelle Wilcox, Pastor Foley, Reverend Donna T'Segaye,
and Reverend Fred Cunningham,
for taking an interest in this project.
We also wish to acknowledge Phil Miller's
kindness for sharing
his network of family and friends.

INTRODUCTION

▼

"Seek ye counsel of the aged, for their eyes have looked on the faces of the years and their ears have hearkened to the voices of life...." (Kahlil Gibran).

This book was written as a tribute to a generation of wise men and women who have experienced life through times of change, wars, depression, peace, pain, and joy. Their strong enduring spirits gave them the courage to cope with death, crisis, and personal struggles. Their wisdom and humor gave them the opportunity to face life with optimism and joy.

We embarked on this project in January of 1998 with open hearts knowing that the seniors with their wisdom and knowledge would provide us with a memorable book. Our interviews included forty-seven men and women from the ages of sixty-nine to one hundred five. Although most of them were from Michigan, we also interviewed people from New Jersey, Texas, Vermont, China, and Nevis in the Caribbean Islands. The diversity (economic levels, religious differences, age differences, experiences, and philosophies) of the people we interviewed showed us that when it comes to the important issues in life there is an underlying universality of thoughts and feelings.

The seniors gave us a wonderful gift, as they welcomed us into their homes and discussed their ideas and experiences. Their graciousness and openness allowed us the opportunity to look through a window into the past and to share their lives.

As we listened with open minds, we made some remarkable discoveries. We found that many of the women had jobs during their child rearing years and played a significant part in their families' finances. The men were open to questions regarding feelings, emotions, and personal experiences. We were impressed by the number of seniors that are involved in important volunteer work and how they provide each other with a network of support. Seniors continue to be goal oriented, still searching for answers, re-evaluating their own ideas, and in many instances embracing change.

All of our seniors have had life altering experiences. Some have faced the death of a child, a spouse, or had to deal with physical illness and pain. Many of them have had to leave their homes, while some have faced loneliness and depression. They have been stretched and challenged. Yet they have emerged through these experiences as strong human beings who are resourceful, loving, and have a positive outlook. They have seen the frailty of the human condition, still maintain their tolerance and compassion, and continue to believe that each new day is a beautiful gift.

This book was designed to celebrate the lives of the seniors we interviewed and to share with you their experiences. A section was added in the back of the book to provide your family the opportunity to hold onto the memories of your loved one through words and pictures. Our hope is that this book will become a family treasure.

We would like to leave you with one last thought. As many seniors say, "Growing old is not for sissies."

CHAPTER 1

▼

Our contributions affect
the lives of our family,
friends, and our community....
How amazing to know
that what we give
comes back to us tenfold.

What do you believe is you greatest contribution?

When you are helping people you are contributing. I hope that by helping people, they will help someone else and things will be better all the way around. (Gordon French)

*   *   *   *

I just take things more or less as they come along. If I can help someone, I will. I have taken care of sick people. I took care of my father-in-law when he broke his hip. I took care of my mother for fourteen years after my stepfather died. Whoever needed my help, I was willing to give it. (Ethel Cutshall)

*   *   *   *

I think being a good citizen, trying to be a good parent, and encouraging our youth is my greatest contribution. For too many years, I saw the negative side of things. You shouldn't dwell on the negative, you should dwell on the positive things in your life. That is what I spend more time doing today. (Richard Tanner)

*   *   *   *

I contribute through my volunteer work in the church. I started a service group. We knit for the babies. Some of what we make goes somewhere in Kentucky. I bake bread and give a lot away. I give it for birthdays and for someone who has done something nice for me or for someone else. (Esther Miller)

*   *   *   *

My biggest contribution is working with my wife to help our daughters be settled and happy. We have been there for the girls when they wanted us. Now they come forward for their mother and are always right there for me. (Edward Cook Jr.)

*   *   *   *

I have raised successful children. I have a flower garden and everyone around has bulbs from my garden. The bulbs that I have multiply. People say they want some flowers so I give them the bulbs. (Marguerite Balch)

*   *   *   *

My greatest contribution is the time I spend with my family. My grandkids tell me that they are glad that I am here so that they have someone to talk to. My grandchildren and my daughter think that I'm the greatest. I am also in charge of the flowers in the community center. We keep them growing and weeded. I worked on the elections and take care of my granddaughter. Mother lives next door and we're doing things to help each other. (Patricia Henry)

*   *   *   *

My children are my greatest contribution. I think all of them have a good sense of humor. They have seen the way I handle things and they seem to be happy with their own self. (Lois Davis)

*   *   *   *

It is hard to look outside yourself, but from a practical point of view I would say it was my teaching. I have card after card from my former pupils. (Marjorie Pierce)

*   *   *   *

Raising my family is my greatest contribution. I tried to teach my children the right way to live. Now I see my daughter doing the same thing. (Christina Hudson)

*   *   *   *

I think, being a good mother and doing volunteer work is my contribution. I worked for St. Joseph Hospital. It was interesting work and it was nice to be able to comfort people with problems. I worked with families when a patient was being operated on and I consoled them. Later after my husband died, I became a grief mentor in my church for others who had lost a spouse. (Dorothy Hoskin)

*   *   *   *

My greatest contribution was bringing up my children and they have gone on and had children. I can see where the value system has been passed on as their children have had children and the value system still holds. (Connie Pearson)

*   *   *   *

I think it would be raising my son. He went to Western and got a degree in Engineering. I would do things with my son when he was young. I showed him how to build a radio. He is a smart boy. He takes after his mother. He spent four years in the navy and he did a great job and now he has two nice children. (Ralph Turner)

*   *   *   *

I think supporting your community is very important. The Lord blessed me and in turn I must take some of the blessings and do something with them. In other words, why should I be the positive force that would take some of the gravy and not pass it along? (Robert Van Blarcom)

*   *   *   *

Well, I guess being the head of the family, keeping us all together, and keeping things cool is my contribution. My wife really does more of the organizational stuff than I do. She does the planning for the get-togethers and weddings. We bought a cottage for the kids and grandkids. Now that they are all over the country we are able to reunite in the summer and spend time together. (Jack Streidl)

*　　　*　　　*　　　*

I think my greatest contribution is to have a good family with good children. I've had a very happy life and I've laughed a lot. (Phil Miller)

*　　　*　　　*　　　*

That is all I ever did was help people. I laugh, I talk, and I treat everyone nice. I do volunteer work at the senior center. I clean the tables, work in the kitchen, and help serve the food. I clean the whole place and wash everything. I am the last one to leave. I have been working there five days a week since 1992. (Ellree Evans)

*　　　*　　　*　　　*

I just did anything I could for anyone that needed it. If I was free, I would do it for them. I think people appreciate that. In clubs or in the school PTA, instead of bringing one thing, I would bring two or three. (Hilda Wesseling)

*　　　*　　　*　　　*

I think my greatest contribution is teaching children, little children. I think that is one of the most wonderful things a women can do in a Sunday School situation. I think it is very important. I am sewing seeds. It is amazing how so many of the graduates in high school now were in my kindergarten class in Sunday school. (Elaine TenBrink)

*　　　*　　　*　　　*

My greatest contribution is influencing young lives through teaching public school and teaching Sunday School. I contributed by just being a good friend to everyone. I am there when people need me. (Ruth McCaw)

*   *   *   *

I think teaching was my contribution. I think the kids liked me and I know that they turned out pretty well. Also, I ran two households. My mother had a limited income so I took and set mother down and showed her my checkbook and she accepted my help. (Elizabeth Purchase)

*   *   *   *

My greatest contribution was raising my Children. They are not owned by parents. When they grow up they will contribute themselves to the world. (Geng, Zheng)

*   *   *   *

Shirley and I visit the elderly people in the nursing homes and elsewhere. I find it gratifying doing something for somebody other than myself and my family. This is one of my contributions. (Dan Hendriksen)

*   *   *   *

I work in the community. I work with the Kalamazoo Habitat for Humanities and I have been with them since 1986. I also work with the Northside Non-Profit Housing Association, the church, the Ministry of Community, and the Kalamazoo NAACP. I am a member of the FEMA board and I did the tax work for the AARP for over 8 years. (Harold Bulger Jr.)

*   *   *   *

I just try to be a cheerful person. When I travel around the world, I give the impression of an American who is interested in their country. I have a good attitude. (Ray Miller)

*   *   *   *

My biggest contribution is the education of the children. When children grow up they will serve the family, but even more they will serve the community. (Wu, Xiugang)

CHAPTER 2

▼

Love is the essence of our soul....
When given unconditionally
it enriches the lives of
all who receive it.

What does love mean to you?

Love is everything in the world that is good. You know, it is the love that is in your family and that you have for friends. (Gertrude Martin)

*   *   *   *

Love means acceptance of each other and knowing that you believe in each other. It is ongoing, not that you don't run into problems. Our love was never questioned. Our love was strong and lasting and could take anything that came along. I always knew that my wife would support me and that things would work out. (Robert Applegate)

*   *   *   *

Love is working together and believing in each other. (Maryetta Lesniak)

*   *   *   *

Love is caring about other people and wanting to be with them. It is being kind to other people, having close friends, and sharing a good relationship at home with your husband. (Millicent Fouchey)

*   *   *   *

When my wife and I got married, we had a wonderful passionate feeling for one another. We worked together all day long and cooperated with each other. (Phil Miller)

*   *   *   *

Love to me means putting someone else's needs in front of your own. (Rosadelle Perry)

*   *   *   *

What does love mean … a million things. Love is a give and take situation where two people agree to have affection for each other. (Connie Pearson)

*   *   *   *

Love, the Bible says, "Love one another as you love yourself." I love a lot of people. I love my kids, the aunts and uncles. I say, "I love people." (Ellree Evans)

*   *   *   *

Love is an all embracing activity that covers all the areas of our lives. Genuine love is best described in the Bible. (George Vargish)

*   *   *   *

It is unselfishness, forgetting self, generosity, kindness, and security. That is the way I felt when my husband was around. I just felt safe and secure. This has been a hard time without him because he was my harbor. (Esther Miller)

*   *   *   *

Love is the biggest thing of all. It makes the world go around. If you don't have love in your heart, you don't have anything. (Ethel Cutshall)

*   *   *   *

It is interesting that you would ask me this. I hesitate to use the word because it is misunderstood and misused. My reasoning on that is the way people talk today. They just love that color, that car, that music, that flower. To me that is the wrong use of that word. In the Hebrew language there are forty different words that are used for love. In our language, we use that one word for everything. I have trouble with that. (Richard Tanner)

*   *   *   *

The word love nowadays is very common. Everyone says it to their children all the time. You love me, I love you. It is a common word. In reality, without the true meaning of the word, my wife and I wouldn't have had over fifty years together. (Tyrus Fouchey)

*   *   *   *

Love is respect, feeling comfortable with another person, feeling more than comfortable. I think it is a feeling on a different plane. Devotion, I don't know, it is hard to define it. It is just something special. When it is there, it makes you feel wonderful. (Lois Davis)

*   *   *   *

Love is hard to explain. Sex doesn't have anything to do with love. It is like the frosting on the cake. Love is respecting the person and feeling that you couldn't live without them. (Ralph Turner)

*   *   *   *

Love means being close. It means loyalty most of all, I think. It doesn't mean that you have to worship anyone but that they always come first and you always feel that you want them to. (Evelyn Moore)

*   *   *   *

Love is a mutual thing. I don't think that love can be one-sided, particularly when you're talking about love with an individual. It has to be reciprocal. That, I feel is the key. I don't get into the love of animated things, such as the love of money, the love of golf. I'm not into that love at all. (Harold Bulger Jr.)

*   *   *   *

Love means understanding your mate. He might be different than you are but you just take him as he is with his ideas, gentleness and faithfulness. Don't try to change him. Love him just as he is. (Dorothy Hoskin)

*   *   *   *

Well, I have always known that God is love. God made us out of love and since love made us, our whole life, should be about love. Whatever we do should come out of love. (Alba "Polly" Pollard)

*   *   *   *

Well it means that you care a lot for someone and you like to do things with them. I think love is very important. If you haven't got love in your heart, you are kind of out of luck. (Hilda Wesseling)

*   *   *   *

Well, I guess it is the feeling of closeness. True love is when you would give up your life for that person. I regard my wife and children that way. (Jack Streidl)

*   *   *   *

Passion about your relationships, passion about your children, passion about music, art, and books, that true deep passionate feeling is love. (Beth Sambo)

*   *   *   *

To tell the truth, I try to love everybody . Of course, you don't love everybody the same. I love my friends. It is easy to love your friends. It is loving your enemy that is hard. (Laculia Byrd)

*   *   *   *

Love means that the children respect their parents. The husband loves the wife. The parents care about the children. With all the love, the road will be easier. I will never care about the toughness of life, you know the hard work, the tiredness. With love you never feel tired. (Wu, Xiugang)

*   *   *   *

I love my children. I had three children and brought them up. I worked very hard to bring them up and give them all a good education. This is a great result of love. (Geng, Zheng)

*   *   *   *

I think love is almost a one word definition, respect. It is more than saying I love you. I don't think that you need to say I love you, but if you're going to say it, mean it. (Elizabeth Purchase)

*   *   *   *

There are many, many meanings for the word love. Some is affection, some is love. I love being here and enjoying God's beauty. That is one kind of love. Then, I dearly love my family and that is another kind of love. Above all, I think the love of God takes precedence. (Ruth McCaw)

*   *   *   *

What is most important to me is God's love. I learned way back when I was a child going to Sunday School, that love is serving others. (Elaine TenBrink)

*   *   *   *

Love means caring and feeling for mankind. You love your kids and you love people. (Florence Atkins)

CHAPTER 3

▼

Death is the final
performance of our lives....
Dying is a process
that can bring us to a place of acceptance.

What are your thoughts on death and dying?

I used to be afraid of death because of my religious upbringing. I was taught that if you have one sin that is not forgiven, you can't go to heaven. That just frightened me right out of the church. Also, I just didn't believe that it could be true. Right now, I'm not afraid of dying, not at all afraid of it. In fact, I have read all about death and what happens afterwards and I have not found anything that really frightens me in all the readings. I think if you try to do the best you can, that is about all anyone can do. No one is perfect. No one lives a perfect life. My father-in-law was a doctor and he said he had never seen anybody at the end afraid to die. He said that he never saw any fear when the time came. I thought that was very interesting. (Esther Miller)

*   *   *   *

I am not afraid of death. It doesn't scare me. When my time comes, I will welcome it. I am not ready to go yet. I want to make sure my children are happy. I want to make sure that they don't have any regrets after I die. I don't want them to feel bad. Really death is just a natural thing that everyone goes through, but I don't feel my time is here yet. (Evelyn Moore)

*   *   *   *

My mother lived to be 94 years old. She had several things happen to her and she asked why the good Lord didn't take her. She said she had a full life. I feel the same way. I don't really want to suffer and I don't want to be a burden. I just hope that when the good Lord takes me, I will be ready to go. I don't want to be ill for a long time. If I am ill, I want to be mentally alert so that I can tell people how to care for me. (Lois Davis)

*   *   *   *

I am hoping that it will be peaceful. I am not afraid to die but I hope I will live a little longer. I believe I will go to heaven when I die. (Millicent Fouchey)

* * * *

I don't think about it often to be honest with you. I used to wonder, when I was younger and saw people my age now, if they were able to work. I would rather not be living than not be able to do the things that I enjoy. That is what bothers me. This stroke I had, it limits me. I don't like to be limited. But I have been fortunate, I am better than a lot of men my age. I don't have very many bad habits. I don't drink, I don't smoke, or spit on the sidewalk. (Robert Van Blarcom)

* * * *

Well, I don't know. I know it happens to everybody. Of course you are not anxious for it to happen to you. I say everybody wants to go to heaven, but no one wants to die. (Laculia Byrd)

* * * *

I have no fear of dying. I figure that the afterlife is going to be okay. If I believed in reincarnation, I'd come back as a sparrow because sparrows get along with the other birds at the feeder. I would come back as a bird because I would enjoy the freedom of flight. I have told my children, that if they see a bird, talk to it, it could be me. (Patricia Henry)

* * * *

I believe that dying is the transformation from this life to another life. (Tyrus Fouchey)

* * * *

I do not have the slightest reluctance to die. (Phil Miller)

*   *   *   *

I look forward to dying a natural death. I'm lonely with my wife being gone. Eternal life is your children, how they live, how they look at life, and what they can accomplish. I have lived my life the best I can. (Robert Applegate)

*   *   *   *

I guess I feel like Woody Allen when he said, "I don't mind dying, I just don't want to be there." I think that death is a natural part of life. I think so often about the statement that Robert Frost made in an interview. They asked him what his philosophy of life was. He thought a minute and said, "I can answer that in three words. It goes on." I think that is good because life does go on, with or without us. (Richard Tanner)

*   *   *   *

I am ready to go anytime to join the Lord. (Dorothy Hoskin)

*   *   *   *

It is quite simple, everyone is going to die if they like it or not. Most people don't want to face it or think about it. On the other hand, you have to think about it because there are a lot of decisions that the family will have to make at the time and they need to know how you feel. The whole area is kind of confusing to me. We don't have enough evidence to know what happens when you die. A lot of people envision going to heaven and really enjoying whatever the afterlife is. I can't picture it. Someday I am going to go there. All I can do is to get ready and let the people know what I want done. (Gordon French)

*   *   *   *

Well no, I'm not afraid of it. I guess you have to decide if you think you have done everything that you wanted to do. I have read all the books I wanted to read and listened to all the music. No, I don't have any fear of it. I don't know what happens after death. (Beth Sambo)

*   *   *   *

It doesn't bother me. It doesn't bother me because I have had such a good life. I have no regrets. No regrets in my lifetime. I have had a beautiful life. (Lillie King Scott)

*   *   *   *

We all have thoughts on dying. Just make sure your will is made. (Ray Miller)

*   *   *   *

I am reading a book called "One Year to Live." It is very interesting. It is about spending a year of your life at any age thinking about what you would do if this was the last year you had. I think the older you get, the more life prepares you to die. I think the only thing that I don't fear is death. The only thing we fear is how it is going to be. We fear the pain. (Phyllis Streidl)

*   *   *   *

Well, I don't want to die until the Lord wants me. I'm going to be ninety-six in August. My mother was ninety-eight and she died in her sleep. My grandma was ninety-nine years old and she could still thread a needle. She had her own teeth, smoked a pipe, and had a droplet of wine every night. (Ralph Turner)

*   *   *   *

Dying is but another phase of our lives. My personal conviction is that just to live on planet earth is a great gift from God. I believe in the promise of another life. (George Vargish)

*   *   *   *

You never know. You try to be ready. That's the reason I treat people the way I want to be treated. I tell folks, you treat people like you want to be treated and God will bless you. (Ellree Evans)

*   *   *   *

I think about it and then I say to myself that I have done everything that I wanted to do. So, it doesn't matter. I'm ready. (Viola Weber)

*   *   *   *

Well, I know that when you get older that it is inevitable. I don't think it is going to happen to me, at least for awhile. (Al Lukeman)

*   *   *   *

I think about death. I think everybody does to a certain extent. We hate to leave our world here but you know, I am anxious to see my husband again. It is hard to think about leaving people and all the things you have worked so hard for. Of course, that isn't much to leave when you think about what a beautiful place we are going to have when we get to heaven. (Hilda Wesseling)

*   *   *   *

Well, I know it is going to happen. It happens to everyone. I know that it's not only in the future, but it is more in the immediate future than I would like to think. I believe that there is a hereafter and I await that. (Dan Hendriksen)

*   *   *   *

Dying is part of life. We are born to die. Therefore we must live with death and with the knowledge that it is going to come. It is a passage. I taught my students a song years ago and the words always come, "I love life and I want to live." Life, there is such a difference between living and existing. God put us here for a purpose. (Alba "Polly" Pollard)

*   *   *   *

I don't think about dying. I just ask God to take care of me because he has the power. I'm not ready to die. The Lord will know when, so I don't bother about it. (Florence Atkins)

*   *   *   *

Well yes, I think about dying but I am not afraid. Heaven is a beautiful place. Many of my family and friends are up there and I hope to meet them again one of these days. (Ruth McCaw)

CHAPTER 4

▼

How we responded in the past
is insignificant....
What lessons we have learned
and how we use them
in the present defines our character.

What lessons has life taught you?

I learned to love unconditionally. After giving birth to seven children and raising them with values, they knew if they went beyond these values that it still didn't diminish my love for them. (Connie Pearson)

*   *   *   *

I have learned not to take things so seriously. I think that I was the worst worrier. I would try to plan way ahead so that everything would come out right. Now I know to take it easy and enjoy life as you go along. (Evelyn Moore)

*   *   *   *

Determination sounds pretty strong. Focus is a good word. Having a goal and insistently make progress toward that goal. I think I have been determined to go ahead and do something with my life. I think you have to have a goal and put aside any arguments against achieving it. I think I was challenged to do well. (Marjorie Pierce)

*   *   *   *

My father was a completely good, honest man. My mother was a completely good, honest woman. I believe that they taught me to be honest. If there is anything that is necessary for success in business, it is honesty. You don't have to tell people that you are honest. Once you have dealt with them for a time there is no way to deceive them. (Phil Miller)

*   *   *   *

I learned to be patient. Sometimes you get upset and think, "Why didn't this go right or that go right?" When you sit down and think about it, things usually do work out in the end. (Ethel Cutshall)

*   *   *   *

I have learned that if you want something in life, you have to sacrifice to do it. If you are not willing to do that, you probably are not going to succeed. (Robert Van Blarcom)

*   *   *   *

I think the most important lesson that I have learned is to overlook the things that you hear other people say about or against you. You need to try to forgive and forget. My greatest hurt is when someone says something about me that is not true. I could never figure out why people would do such a thing. It is a lesson in forgiveness and I try to forgive. (Al Lukeman)

*   *   *   *

I have learned that if you are kind to people, they will be kind to you. (Lorita Powell)

*   *   *   *

Well you have to take things as they come and even though you get upset, you have to know that everything passes and that things will get better. Try to keep looking at the bright side rather than worrying all the time. (Millicent Fouchey)

*   *   *   *

I want to say, don't sweat the little things, but the little things can become mountains. So just remember that tomorrow is always better. (Patricia Henry)

*   *   *   *

I think honesty is very, very important. Well, I just think there are many people who help themselves to other people's things. If it doesn't belong to you, leave it alone. (Hilda Wessling)

*   *   *   *

Always be kind to people, pay attention to them, and enjoy them. (Gertrude Martin)

*   *   *   *

I try to remember 'This to shall pass'. Things can be pretty bad, but you know that they are not permanent and always, there is a way out. I think that is the most important lesson. There have been a lot of lessons, of course, not just one. I was raised that we always have work to do. I shall never be too old for it or too feeble. Every day that dawns brings something special to do. I think God put us on this earth and it is up to us to find out what our purpose is. (Esther Miller)

*   *   *   *

Be patient and be honest. I hope that I have always been honest. (Christina Hudson)

*   *   *   *

I have learned so many lessons and I still have a lot to learn. I think I have found over the years that I have been one to ask everyone else their opinion of something before I would decide what mine was. After I retired, I decided that I needed to work on my own opinion first and not worry about what anyone else thought. I have always sought advice and counsel and now I use my own. (Richard Tanner)

*   *   *   *

Oh, I guess I go with the flow, not getting too high or too low because you have to take the good thing with the problems. So, I suppose it is sort of like coaching. We say that you're going to hit the heights of acceleration and the depths of despair. We tell the players to try to keep an even keel so that you don't feel too good when things are going good or too bad when things are going wrong. (Jack Streidl)

*   *   *   *

Life has taught me to be patient, to keep going, and don't ever give up. Many difficult things happen and you could give up very easily. So, I just felt that I had to keep going and do the best I could do in every situation. (Elaine TenBrink)

*   *   *   *

I learned one thing and that is when you are faced with adversities you have to turn them around so they become opportunities. Go through them, correct them, and you will be a better person. (Gordon TenBrink)

*   *   *   *

Life itself is one big lesson and the lessons just come automatically. (Tyrus Fouchey)

*   *   *   *

The most important thing is that when something goes wrong, don't sweat it. If you have a problem there are a number of solutions. Don't come up with just one solution. Come up with a plan that is good, then come up with plan b and plan c and rank them in order. Then if one doesn't work, you don't get upset because you have a backup plan. I think the way the mind works is that if you put too much stress on it, you get nowhere. If you really define a problem and come up with a solution, let it rest for awhile. Relax, give the brain time to work things out before you act. (Gordon French)

*   *   *   *

The most important lesson I have learned, through my experiences in life, is to get along with everyone. When you have a job to do, you need to be nice to people and they will respond positively to you. (Paul Dreer)

*   *   *   *

The most important lesson is to trust in God. Sometimes faith lessens, but you have to continue on and talk to God. Then things will get better. God put me here for a purpose and I'm still trying to fulfill that purpose. (Ruth McCaw)

*   *   *   *

You usually get what you give. You can't give love if you don't have love in your heart. So therefore you start with yourself. Loving yourself but not in an arrogant way. Then do what you can with what you have. (Alba "Polly" Pollard)

*   *   *   *

I have learned the importance of being independent. I have learned to do things on my own. I believe that is important in life. (Viola Weber)

*   *   *   *

You just have to stay calm and keep going. You can't just cave in or knuckle under. I have had a lot of challenges and I could have done that, but I didn't. Someone had to be strong so I was the one, I guess. (Beth Sambo)

*   *   *   *

Being older and hopefully wiser, I feel that the pen is more powerful than the sword. I believe more can be achieved during peace than in war. I have learned that freedom is a gift, but it does have a price. (Gordon TenBrink)

*   *   *   *

Well, I tell you the biggest thing is to treat people like you want to be treated. Only seldom do I loose my temper when a person slashes out. My husband is a very tolerant person and I have learned from him. (Lillie King Scott)

*   *   *   *

Never quit. I always fight to achieve the mission of that period in my life. I always put forth the greatest effort. (George Vargish)

*   *   *   *

I have learned to laugh at how things are. Everything seems so important when you are younger. When you get older you wonder why you were so worried about certain things. (Ray Miller)

*   *   *   *

I like to think about the words that my father passed on to me. When I asked him what his philosophy was in life, he said, "It is very simple, treat yourself right and treat the next man better than you treat yourself." I thought about it for a long time. It is so simple, it is so obvious. If you follow this philosophy, you'll always get along with others. (Harold Bulger Jr.)

*   *   *   *

Well for one thing, I learned to keep my temper down a little bit. I just learned that I could take a lot of things and still survive. (Laculia Byrd)

*   *   *   *

Well, one thing that I have become convinced about is that the more I learn, the more I realize all the things that I don't know. So, that is a revelation. (Dan Hendricksen)

*   *   *   *

Believe in yourself and the Lord. Now, that is the way I do it. The Lord opens the way for me and I follow. (Florence Atkins)

CHAPTER 5

▼

Never has a generation
experienced so many changes
in one lifetime....
Their ability to accept these changes and move forward
is a tribute to their determination,
resourcefulness, and vision.

What are your thoughts about the changes that you have experienced in your lifetime?

I think we are at the beginning of a real fascinating era. I see so many changes to come particularly in the areas of science, biology, and chemistry of the human body. We are making a good start with DNA investigations which are giving us information regarding single cell reproduction. They are just beginning to understand areas of the brain. (Gordon French)

*   *   *   *

We live in an altogether different world than we used to. It is not the same, so much tension. (Lillie King Scott)

*   *   *   *

When I was young we would wash clothes by hand. We had to plant the seeds and then carry buckets of water into the fields on the farm. We cooked on three stones and used a coal pot. Now we have electricity and water. Thing are much better, but there are still times when our electricity goes out on the Island and we have to cook outside. (Lorita Powell)

*   *   *   *

Well there is so much more cruelty on television than there used to be. TV was enjoyable but not anymore. There is a wrestling match on TV and it is so terrible. They pound one another. I wonder how they put it on television. (Gertrude Martin)

*   *   *   *

We have to be very flexible and adaptable. I find that easy for me, as long as it is an advance and is going forward. (Alba "Polly" Pollard)

*   *   *   *

Well, when you stop and think that I'm 100 years old, I've seen a lot of changes. I was brought up on a farm in Indiana. We didn't have heat and gas in the beginning. The first car that we had was a little red Studebaker. (Lydia Nickerson)

*   *   *   *

I am very happy with all the technological changes. (Edward Cook Jr.)

*   *   *   *

Well, I think growing up was probably simpler back in my day. It's much more complicated now and raising kids is probably tougher. (Jack Streidl)

*   *   *   *

The speed with which we can get from place to place is amazing. The computer has brought about many changes in the way people live. I think economic change is related to social change. Now, everyone in the world is more knowledgeable about what is going on. Hopefully this will help make our world more peaceful and teach us to stay out of wars. (Elizabeth Purchase)

*   *   *   *

I was just talking about all the changes I have lived through the other day. In fact, I was thinking that so much has happened in this century. I feel very fortunate to have lived through it. (Al Lukeman)

*   *   *   *

When I was a young boy in China, I could not sleep peacefully. Later, the war was over. Then people could live and work in peace and contentment. This is a good thing. This is a good change. (Wu, Xiugang)

*   *   *   *

Yes, I have seen many changes in my lifetime. I have seen the beginning of electric lights, airplanes, and television. There has been many changes in cars, people landing on the moon, telephones, and washing machines. Absolutely, the changes have been good. (Ethel Cutshall)

*   *   *   *

Well, everything changes, everything changes. I would like some things to stay the same sometime. (Laculia Byrd)

*   *   *   *

I see change as positive. I think that using the computer and internet makes t possible to service a much larger community. (Rosadelle Perry)

*   *   *   *

Of course, the technical changes are astounding. I am not as pleased with the social changes. (Richard Tanner)

*   *   *   *

When I think about the world, I think that either I am slowing down or the world is going faster. I can't keep up with all the technology. I don't know if the children have changed or adults have changed. Everyone is so completely busy and I wonder if they put much effort in things of value. There has been so many advances in medicine and business. The good thing is that so much information is right at your fingertips. (Lois Davis)

*   *   *   *

I see some of the changes as being wonderful and they make life easier. Life has gotten better in some regards. (Phyllis Streidl)

*   *   *   *

I think life is more tenuous—I question my own ability to judge it. When you're younger, you don't have concerns about changes. You think of the present, your job, and your children. You start to look at life differently when you are older. (Robert Applegate)

*   *   *   *

Well, they say there has been a revolution in recent years and I think that is quite right. The microchip has revolutionized the world. That is almost overwhelming. In other words, it is not the industrial age anymore, but the technological age. We are in the age of computers, internet, the web, cell phone, e-mail, and CD ROM. The world was definitely more personal before and I think we have lost something. I think people are lonelier today. (Dan Hendriksen)

*   *   *   *

Technology has done a lot for medicine, travel, and the comfort of people. Sometimes, I think maybe we have become too comfortable. When the power goes off we're completely lost. (Ruth McCaw)

*   *   *   *

Sometimes I feel like my mother. She used to say, "Stop the world, I would like to get off." I just can't keep up. You just have to put it out of your mind and accept things that you can not change. I was using a typewriter and then they came up with the word processor, then the computer. I felt like I was too old to learn. Maybe I should have. I could use it today. My children and grandchildren all have computers. (Esther Miller)

*   *   *   *

I remember, we had the first TV in our neighborhood. My dad put it together. With all the changes, things come easier now. (Maryetta Lesniak)

*　　　*　　　*　　　*

Progress, a lot of it I don't like, but you have to go with the flow. I have seen a lot of changes. When I moved here all the streets were gravel and you could count the houses in the area. Now, you can't count all the houses. The traffic is amazing. (Viola Weber)

*　　　*　　　*　　　*

I think all the changes are marvelous. I try to keep up with them all. I would love to see what is going to happen in the 21st century. What we have seen invented from 1900 to 1999 is just amazing. I get on the internet and talk with my daughter. I just flash her and I can talk to her. (Patricia Henry)

CHAPTER 6

▼

When we are faced with
challenges, we have a choice....
We can stay in the valley
or continue our journey
up the mountain.

What has been your greatest challenge?

My greatest challenge was to be a good husband and a good father. I think the most important job in the world is to raise your children properly. My children all treat me very well as a result of me treating them well. They are my greatest satisfaction. (Phil Miller)

*   *   *   *

Well during challenging times it is important to keep your equilibrium. The time I got cancer, when I had Malaria, and being married twice were all life threatening. You try to get above them. (Ray Miller)

*   *   *   *

I suppose raising kids was my greatest challenge. Teaching them to be honest, kind, and care about others was important. (Millicent Fouchey)

*   *   *   *

The most difficult time was when my marriage was terminated. Economically there wasn't anything to fall back on. I came out feeling defeated. Although I had visions of going out and making money, it was difficult with seven kids. I learned to accept that I wasn't going to be wealthy, but I was going to be comfortable on my own. (Connie Pearson)

*   *   *   *

I guess raising my kids. I was married in 1935. My husband and I were together for fifty-seven years before he died. He loved children and I had it all figured out. I was going to have four children, two boys and two girls. We waited. No children, still no children. Yet, we did end up with four children through adoption and family. We had two girls and two boys. (Laculia Byrd)

*   *   *   *

My greatest challenge is not being able to do the things that I want to do so badly. (Gertrude Martin)

*   *   *   *

The most difficult time was after my first husband died. I bought this house. That was the biggest thing that I had ever done on my own. (Lillie King Scott)

*   *   *   *

Personally, during the course of my life it has always been a challenge to get the most out of what I have. In other words, knowing and recognizing my limitations helps me to succeed. (Harold Bulger Jr.)

*   *   *   *

I had not directed an intensive program of any kind. I tend to want to be in the system where I am not the manager or director. I was persuaded to take the directorship of a new program in English for internationals at Western Michigan University in the middle seventy's. That was quite a challenge and after six years I was able to go back to teaching. (Dan Hendriksen)

*   *   *   *

People say the first hundred years are the hardest. I don't think so. I have found that the years past one hundred have been the most challenging. (Gertrude Powell)

*   *   *   *

It was a challenge living through the depression. I had eight children but I didn't have any problem raising them since I had come from a big family. My mother had 12 children. (Marguerite Balch)

*   *   *   *

I think getting the money to go to college to be a teacher was a challenge. I was sure I wanted to be a teacher from the time I was just a little kid. I used to watch the teacher go by our store even before I went to school. I thought, I just have to be a teacher. (Elizabeth Purchase)

*   *   *   *

I believe that God has given each human being a gift. The greatest challenge is knowing how to use it. (George Vargish)

*   *   *   *

Probably the greatest challenge that I had was during the depression. I grew up in a family that was quite prosperous and we lost everything. That was at the time that I was ready to go to college. With the help of God, my sister, and everyone pitching in, I was able to get a college education. (Al Lukeman)

*   *   *   *

Life is a constant challenge. I had an aim in my life. If I decided to do something, I stayed on course and I didn't wander off. I had advantages, I had good friends and a good family. That is important in life to get ahead. (Marjorie Pierce)

*   *   *   *

I think my greatest challenge was showing my horse Wimpy. He was only four years old and I took him to Iowa. I placed in the junior class and then went into the championship class. That is the class that the professionals from all over the states come to show their horses. There were ninety-seven horses there and I won. (Viola Weber)

*   *   *   *

My work. I always liked to write. My writing was good and my photography was excellent. I could get at the feeling of the story. I was a pretty damn good writer and I became more confident as I went along. (Robert Applegate)

*   *   *   *

I would say that it is myself and my relationship with God and humanity. I have always considered that everyone is equal. I believe in doing unto others as I would have them do unto me. (Gordon TenBrink)

*   *   *   *

Well, I suppose it was raising eleven kids and making sure that they all got through college. We lost one daughter, she died. We raised her three kids and they are now out of college and doing pretty well. (Jack Streidl)

*   *   *   *

Working and accomplishing something was a challenge. I had different challenges at different times. When my husband was ill, I just accepted that and did the very best I could. My special needs child could be a challenge, but I never looked at him that way. (Lois Davis)

*   *   *   *

I was born in a generation that expected you to make your marriage work. I was always a doer and a hard worker. So I more or less made sure everything kept going along on an even keel and the right way. (Evelyn Moore)

*   *   *   *

I suppose when my husband died and I had to try to face everything by myself. I just thought that I couldn't do it. Day by day, one day at a time, I always found the courage and the strength to go on. (Esther Miller)

*   *   *   *

Well, my greatest challenge was when I was young and was away from home and my family. I had to count on myself and not depend on anyone. That was kind of hard at first. (Paul Dreer)

*   *   *   *

I think coping with a lot of different types of things. You cope with your spouse, the kids, and things that are going on. You have to stay strong to meet the challenges. (Beth Sambo)

*   *   *   *

It would have to be the death of my daughter and the decision to raise her children. It didn't seem a hard decision at the time. It just needed to be done and we wanted to do it. (Phyllis Streidl)

*   *   *   *

It was a challenge when we decided to write the history of Oakwood. We have lived here for sixty years and have always had an interest in it. We decided we wanted to put the history down on paper. It is such an interesting neighborhood and it goes back to 1829. It was a challenge because there is so much information and you want to get it all down. We hope to have it published some day. (Patricia Henry)

*   *   *   *

My greatest challenge was when I wanted to get married. My parents were Lutheran and at that time there was a great and vast difference in religions. My father thought I should marry a Protestant even though he liked the man I wanted to marry. I told my father that I could not live with him without the man I loved. It ended up that we lived with my parents for three years during the depression, so it all worked out. (Dorothy Hoskin)

*   *   *   *

I think that would be trying to make a new life after my husband died. I was completely lost without his love and affection. So the biggest challenge has been to find myself and to be able to help others. (Ruth McCaw)

*   *   *   *

I think my greatest challenge was showing my horse Wimpy. He was only four years old and I took him to Iowa. I placed in the junior class and then went into the championship class. That is the class that the professionals from all over the states come to show their horses. There were ninety-seven horses there and I won. (Viola Weber)

CHAPTER 7

▼

The greatest strength that
we possess lies within ...
It is the ability to reach deep
inside during a crisis
and find the courage
to overcome our fears.

How do you deal with crisis in your life?

I deal with crisis by not letting myself be hurried into making a decision. Sometimes it seems that events or the people around you are pressuring you to make a decision right now. That can lead to some very serious mistakes. I've been able to discipline myself to wait a little while before I make important decisions in my life. I have also been able to resist peer pressure. I was brought up to believe that I knew what was right and what was wrong and that I should stick to what I believe in. (Rosadelle Perry)

*   *   *   *

I pray. I think I get outside help from prayer. I also have been very fortunate to have people around me who are very supportive. I do have some very dear friends and I just think positive. (Lois Davis)

*   *   *   *

Drive, I just keep going. Knowing that I have to do it, I work it out. (Robert Applegate)

*   *   *   *

I pray a lot. I just try to use good sense and really take it one day at a time. You have to. If you look ahead too far, it is scary. (Phyllis Streidl)

*   *   *   *

I haven't faced many crisis. Once in awhile, I will cry some tears and get in the car and listen to a country western station. Then I can cry my eyes out when I listen to that sad, sad music. I haven't had to do that in a long time. (Patricia Henry)

*   *   *   *

I would evaluate the problem and make two columns. What is good about it and what is bad about it. I tried to be impartial when writing the list. When you get it all done, you summarize the problem and then make a fairly intelligent decision. You always want a back up plan since most of the solutions depend on others. I have dealt with crisis in my life. If things go bad, they will turn around. You just have to have faith. (Gordon French)

*   *   *   *

We adopted two special needs children. Our son was a genius and an athlete. When he was seventeen, he was diagnosed with schizophrenia. He died when he was twenty-nine years old. Our daughter was a diabetic and on insulin and she died at thirty-two. We thank God for giving us both of them. They enriched our lives and made them complete. So we just thank God for placing them in our hands even though we had to give them up. (Gordon TenBrink)

*   *   *   *

Well, I think the first thing is to remain calm and don't get excited. Don't go off half cocked in a direction you are not sure of before you know what is happening or what is causing the disaster. Then, I try to figure out what should be done next. (Richard Tanner)

*   *   *   *

I handle crisis through prayer, praying to God. God has helped me through many, many things. (Ruth McCaw)

*   *   *   *

It depends on what the crisis is and if I have the skills to resolve it. Sometimes I need more information. If there is a crisis, I know I can't run away from it because then I get frustrated and angry. That can lead to depression. I have learned to use the depression as a time-out and go on from there to make some adjustments and new decisions. (Connie Pearson)

*   *   *   *

Like I say, this to shall pass. (Esther Miller)

*   *   *   *

I have had enough of them in my early years. My sister died when I was younger and then my mother died. You can't go back, you have to face it. You have to do the best you can and give it all you got. (Robert Van Blarcom)

*   *   *   *

I realize that there is no way I can change the world and I know that crisis do happen. Instead of letting it get the best of me, I have to get the best of it. I always figure out a way to handle things. Usually, I don't make a snap judgment. I think about it and ponder it. I might talk to someone about it if the opportunity comes up, but I don't go out seeking help. I think about what is the best way to figure things out or what is the best thing to do. I have to figure it out my own way so that I can handle it my way. I rely on myself. My generation is more like that. (Evelyn Moore)

*   *   *   *

Well I haven't had many emergencies. I am very, very lucky. I have been very blessed. When I did have a crisis, I would usually talk to someone. My father passed away first in our family. That was hard for me to accept. I just kept very busy and I liked people around me. (Hilda Wesseling)

*   *   *   *

The formula given to us at an early age was to maintain the moral standards my mother established. When a crisis occurred, prayer was the first step and then to reach out for help if the issue was one requiring a skill I did not possess. (George Vargish)

*　　　*　　　*　　　*

I deal with every crisis that I have experienced through my relationship with God. I am most grateful for my Christian heritage. (Gordon TenBrink)

*　　　*　　　*　　　*

Well, first I crumble inside and then I panic. I let a few days go by and then I try to figure it out. Maybe I talk about it to someone, usually a daughter, son, or a trusted friend. Finally, I sort out what it is that I am going to do about it. Once I figure out what I am going to do and how I am going to handle it, I'm fine. (Beth Sambo)

*　　　*　　　*　　　*

Most of the things I thought were a crisis turned out to be a benefit. Like the time I was caught during the war. After I was captured by the Germans, I was put inside a barbed wire fence where I was completely safe and no one was shooting at me. My child had a son born with Down Syndrome and I thought that was a terrible tragedy. Now he is thirty-one years old and the most popular kid in the family. My grandson, everyone wants to be with him. I can't think of anything that was a great problem that didn't turn out to be a benefit. I don't have any regrets and I don't have any complaints. (Phil Miller)

*　　　*　　　*　　　*

I deal with crisis in my life by meeting it head on. My wife, Phyllis and I are both the same with respect to the cup being half full instead of half empty. We always look at the bright side of things. So, we are generally able to handle most any crisis. (Jack Streidl)

*　　　*　　　*　　　*

I just kept going and kept doing the best that I can. Sometimes you just have to get through a crisis. I just prayed to God that I would be able to handle it. (Elaine TenBrink)

*   *   *   *

I had a wife that was very ill. She passed away and we had three little children. I was able to raise them and keep them together. I had determination. I knew that it had to be done. (Al Lukeman)

*   *   *   *

My worst crisis was the death of my parents, brothers, and sister. I did have family to help. I had to get through it on my own. (Marjorie Pierce)

*   *   *   *

If I have a crisis, I take off into the woods. I get away from the problem by pruning trees. I then use self-psychology to help myself. (Edward Cook Jr.)

CHAPTER 8

▼

The younger generation will hold
the world in their hands....
We wish them freedom, understanding, compassion,
vision, and peace.

What words do you have for the younger generation?

Appreciate what you have and do the most with it. The opportunities are fantastic. Gain as much knowledge as you can and take care of yourself. (Lois Davis)

*   *   *   *

They should try to look ahead a couple of years and say, "Where do I want to be? Now, how do I get there?" The only way you are going to get there is to put your eye on your goal and never take it off. If you work at it, you will succeed. (Robert Van Blarcom)

*   *   *   *

If you have something on your mind that you want to do, then make a success of it. That is the way I was brought up and that is the way I brought my children up. When you start something, you have to finish it. My father didn't care what we did as long as we stuck with it and made a success of it. (Ethel Cutshall)

*   *   *   *

Don't be afraid to be yourself. There are going to be times when you are being yourself and people will laugh at you. I have had that happen. It never deterred me. I knew I had to be myself, because I had to live with myself. You can't pretend. Just be yourself and enjoy life. Also, don't think that you have to conquer the world. Just do the best you can and be happy with what level you do achieve. (Evelyn Moore)

*   *   *   *

I think being a teenager is a hard, hard age but it doesn't last. It is only temporary. They are going through a period of change and it is important for them to know that. They are not always going to feel the way they do now. They have to be careful that they don't make mistakes that they will regret the rest of their lives. I think that it is important for them to be a part of a group in church. It is a wonderful experience and gives them a sense of belonging. (Esther Miller)

*   *   *   *

My message to today's youth is to be absolutely honest in everything that you do. Be true to yourself and never expect something for nothing. (Phil Miller)

*   *   *   *

I want to impart to them to be true, honest, helpful to others, love God, and go to church. Be of service to others and live a clean life. I feel sorry for today's youth. The problem is that we hear about the bad things that they do and we don't hear about the good things. There are many, many young people that are living a religious life, helping other people, and trying to make the world a better place. (Ruth McCaw)

*   *   *   *

Get along with others and don't let things bother you. There is always a way out. If something bothers you, do something about it. (Maryetta Lesniak)

*   *   *   *

I had a boy talk to me the other day and he was in the first grade. I was amazed at how smart he was and how he could talk. Sometimes, I like to listen to them because they tell me not to sweat the small stuff. They will have a lot of high mountains to climb but they will have many chances to get to the top. (Pat Henry)

*   *   *   *

I think that it is up to each generation to make a better life for themselves. (Tryus Fouchey)

*   *   *   *

I taught my seven children that you have to take responsibility for your actions. That is what I would pass on to the younger generation. (Connie Pearson)

*   *   *   *

Listen to yourself, not what your elders would tell you because the world is changing and I'll be damned if I would preach to the youth. You will solve your problems just like I did by meeting them head on. (Robert Applegate)

*   *   *   *

Be strong enough to follow a path that you believe is right no matter what anyone else thinks of it. Develop good work ethics. (Rosadelle Perry)

*   *   *   *

Be honest, truthful, and respect the laws. (Ralph Turner)

*   *   *   *

You need to learn math and science. You can't make intelligent decisions without background information. Science teaches you to question things and to try to revise methods to check what you are doing and to make sure you are on the right track. (Gordon French)

*   *   *   *

I wish, I just hope that they have peace in the world and that the young people find themselves and have a wonderful life. For my children, I hope that they continue to live a happy life. (Millicent Fouchey)

*   *   *   *

I guess I would want to encourage them to explore every possible potential. Don't waste time on junk. Experience everything you can. (Beth Sambo)

*   *   *   *

Love your mother and father, they gave you life. That is what we tell our grand-children. (Paul Dreer)

*   *   *   *

First, teach the children to study a lot. Study is always good for them. Second, encourage the children to help each other. Third, encourage them if they have problems to talk with their parents. (Wu, Xiugang)

*   *   *   *

Never give up. (Elaine TenBrink)

*   *   *   *

I think the most important thing is just be kind to each other and to have a focus in your life. I realize now and think how important it is to know what you want to do with your life early on. Not many do. They just wait and see what happens. I talked with my granddaughter yesterday who wanted to get into graduate school and she is bemoaning the fact that she didn't work as hard as she could in college. She was content to get by with just B's. She wished she had hung in there and worked harder. I couldn't have told her that at that time, but she knows it now. (Phyllis Streidl)

*   *   *   *

Parents need to know what children are thinking. They are always curious and sometimes their actions are impulsive. For such children, the grownups should observe them to know them. Let them know what will happen if they do something so they understand. Advise them to think about their future. Encourage them to make a bright future, and to do something else to make their life different. Love them. (Geng, Zheng)

*   *   *   *

I would just like to see teenagers reading more and talking more to adults. (Ray Miller)

*   *   *   *

Stay off drugs. Be interested in God, church work, and helping people. (Hilda Wesseling)

*   *   *   *

My message would be to parents rather than children. Parents need to come together to make decisions. (Marjorie Pierce)

*   *   *   *

Today's youth, my first advice is to be true to yourself and your creator. If you are true to yourself, you will be true to others. Don't try to fulfill the worldly desires and the desires of the flesh. Relate to those things that are of true value—honesty, integrity, and morality. (Gordon TenBrink)

*   *   *   *

I think young people should take marriage seriously. (Lydia Nickerson)

*   *   *   *

Well, I think they need to have some kind of ideal or goal in their life that motivates them. They need to think for themselves as much as possible and they need to contribute something to society. Also, I think that a belief in a higher power is very important. (Dan Hendriksen)

CHAPTER 9

▼

Happiness is the substance
of our lives....
When we spend our time trying
to create it,
we miss the very moments
that we are searching for.

What makes you happy?

It makes me happy to see the success of my children. Also, to have my grandchildren read the paper to me at night. (Phil Miller)

*   *   *   *

I'm happy when the sun is out and everybody is in a good mood. (Lois Davis)

*   *   *   *

Accomplishing something makes me happy. If a day goes by that I don't accomplish something, I get depressed. I think that being active and doing something for someone else really makes you feel appreciative. When someone wants to pay me back, I say, "Don't take away my gift." (Esther Miller)

*   *   *   *

I try real hard not to let life get me down. I've had problems but I try to survive them. Physical difficulties come with age. I have to have my mind focused on other things. I love to read and I have a stamp collection. I have an autograph collection, a small coin collection, and a bottle collection. I like being around people, especially children. (Marjorie Pierce)

*   *   *   *

It makes me happy to see my children happy. (Dorothy Hoskin)

*   *   *   *

Many things make me happy. I enjoy going out or staying at home with family and friends. I find happiness in everyday things. I love to laugh. (Millicent Fouchey)

*   *   *   *

Happiness is when I married my wife. (Ralph Turner)

*   *   *   *

Just life, a nice sunny day when you are going out, that is instrumental. I enjoy having a good dinner. These things are all part of life and they make me happy. (Tyrus Fouchey)

*   *   *   *

We have to help each other. It is in helping other people that gives you the best rewards. (Gordon French)

*   *   *   *

Seeing your kids grow-up and develop made me happy. Also, seeing my business grow made me happy. I bought one lumber yard and I bought a second one. I didn't do it for the money itself because money is not my god. I liked making a successful organization. (Robert Van Blarcom)

*   *   *   *

I probably would have to say family makes me happy. When the girls were growing up and my daughter was six months old, I would take her to work with me and I would change her diapers, and give her the bottle. I made the equipment in the back seat of the car so she would not fall off the seat. We took vacations and nursed the girls through a lot. I also find happiness living on one hundred acres and getting away from problems by growing Christmas trees. (Edward Cook Jr.)

*   *   *   *

Just seeing my family or when they call me, that makes me happy. (Christina Hudson)

*   *   *   *

I was fortunate enough to have a good marriage. My greatest pleasures involve family. (Rosadelle Perry)

*   *   *   *

I enjoy my family. I like to go bowling. These days, I don't usually score one hundred, but today I made one hundred and thirty-five. (Laculia Byrd)

*   *   *   *

My grandchildren make me happy. I like working in the garden in the spring time. I like to plant things and watch them grow. I enjoy thinking, writing, and taking pictures. I like to deal with feelings rather than dealing with facts. I have a lovely dog, sweetest dog, who understands when I am down. He is the most loving animal that I have ever had. My wife is gone and I spend a lot of time with him. He is very responsive to my feelings. (Robert Applegate)

*   *   *   *

I am usually a happy person. Like I told my husband, I have been happy all my life and nobody is going to kill my joy. He never did anything to upset me. (Lillie King Scott)

*   *   *   *

People getting along, family, and lots of loving make me happy. (Maryetta Lesniak)

*   *   *   *

Out here, it is just guys dropping over and having a beer, that sort of thing. Just being with people in conversation makes me happy. Then when you are by yourself, you appreciate people even more. (Ray Miller)

*   *   *   *

Well, I'm crazy about all sports. I watch an awful lot of sports and go to all the high school games here. I go to all of Western's football games. I am happy with family and when we socialize with our kids and have dinner, that sort of thing. I'm happy being around my wife all the time. (Jack Striedl)

*   *   *   *

The biggest thing that makes me happy is observing my son, his wife, and his son. I guess I get my biggest happiness out of observing my family. (Harold Bulger Jr.)

*   *   *   *

I love cooking. I love making a home. I am an avid reader and an avid gardener. I love children, music, books, and gardening. (Beth Sambo)

*   *   *   *

Happiness lies in the pursuit of helping others who are in need. The giving of ourselves generates the greatest rewards. (George Vargish)

*   *   *   *

Oh, to be around people makes me happy. I love my family. I have four grand-sons, four great-grandsons, and nine little great, great-grandchildren. They make me happy. They are lovely. (Gertrude Martin)

*   *   *   *

Talking, laughing, and enjoying good people, that is what makes me happy. (Ellree Evans)

*   *   *   *

I ride my horse. I ride a couple times a week. Taking care of him and my dog is my enjoyment. I get up in the morning and feed them. That is my reason for getting out of bed. (Viola Weber)

*   *   *   *

I enjoy making people happy and doing things for others. Company makes me happy. (Hilda Wesseling)

*   *   *   *

My children are a source of joy. I couldn't have asked for anything more. Also, my husband and I traveled a lot. We took the railroad because we had passes from his job. Later we traveled to Europe on tours. Well, I was so contented and happy when we moved to Climax. It was home from the time we moved in. Everybody was so nice to us and my children went to school here. (Lydia Nickerson)

*   *   *   *

Just being alive makes me happy. I love to smile. I had a big sign on my wall when I worked at Western which said, "If you see someone without a smile, give them one of yours. It always comes back to you." (Alba "Polly" Pollard)

*   *   *   *

My marriage, friends, and children make me happy. (Phyllis Streidl)

*   *   *   *

I'm most happy when I'm helping somebody. That's why I'm doing all the work that I do because I feel that am helping others. That's my biggest joy in life. I'm sure that Jesus put me on Earth to help other people. (Ruth McCaw)

* * * *

I have always been a sportsman and I hunted and fished. I have had a cottage, snowmobiles, a horse, and a dog. Those make me happy. Also when I am contributing to others, it always comes back to me. When you give, you get back. (Gordon TenBrink)

* * * *

I enjoy life. I enjoyed marrying my wife. The biggest thing in my life now is my wife, my kids, my grandchildren and great grand-children, my family. I enjoy people. (Paul Dreer)

* * * *

Children make me happy. I like to garden, plant food, and go out and pick vegetables. I like listening to songs and watching TV. I like steel drums and string bands, the Island music. (Lorita Powell)

* * * *

Beautiful women have always made me happy. I think friends and friendships make me happy. I enjoy the little children in the neighborhood. It is obvious that they like me. They call me Al. (Al Lukeman)

* * * *

My son David is the joy of my life. My daughter-in-law and the children have been so good to me. (Gertrude Powell)

* * * *

A good wife, good children, and good grandchildren make me happy. (Wu, Xiugang)

*   *   *   *

Oh, I think being retired and not having the pressure of the job makes me happy. I do work part-time, but it is not the same. I don't have to be at the job at a certain time or meet deadlines. I can work more or less on my own time. That is a relief. I also enjoy travel. We have a daughter in California so that is an enjoyment. (Dan Hendriksen)

*   *   *   *

Whenever children come around me, I am happy. (Geng, Zheng)

*   *   *   *

Happiness is when there are people around who I can talk with and when little children are around. (Marguerite Balch)

*   *   *   *

Life makes me happy. There are so many good things that I enjoy. I'm happy with friends. I enjoy travel, good food, music, theater, and plays. (Elizabeth Purchase)

*   *   *   *

Watching my grandchildren grow makes me happy. (Ethel Cutshall)

CHAPTER 10

▼

Once we have experienced
a miracle, we are never the same....
Our heart is open to
extraordinary possibilities.

Have you experienced any miracles in your life?

Yes, I think so. One thing in particular stands out in my mind. We had taken my father to the hospital for treatment of cancer. It was spreading. My mother was not well enough to go to the hospital so my husband and I would stay at night with my mother. When I got out of work, my husband took me in the afternoon to visit my father. My father seemed no worse than he had been and he ate a good meal. The next day, I don't know where the message came from, but I knew that my father was very critical. I was so compelled to go to the hospital that I left right away. My husband couldn't understand the urgency. When I got there, I found out that the treatment to stop the cancer was ruining his bone marrow. The doctor had ordered that the blood transfusions be stopped. I held my father's hand and read from the Bible and he died shortly after midnight. Even though I was away from him, I knew he was dying. I am sure that the Lord spoke to me and told me what to do. (Rosadelle Perry)

*   *   *   *

Well, yes. I think planting a seed and watching it grow is a miracle. I have had a garden for years and have grown trees and the things that happen in nature that we all take for granted. In my view, they are miracles. They really are. Also, things in our body are a miracle. Well, I think life itself is a miracle. (Richard Tanner)

*   *   *   *

About 30 years ago, I came down with a sickness. My friends came to visit me. Everyone doubted that I could live. I did. I made it. It was a miracle. (Geng, Zheng)

*   *   *   *

We look for them, don't we? I think they come in small ways so that you don't recognize them as such. Life has been good and every once in awhile there is something that happens so well that you can think of it that way. Just being alive, healthy, and happy is a miracle. (Patricia Henry)

*   *   *   *

The fact that a women's body can conceive and grow and give birth to a whole human being, that is incredible. Each and every child was my miracle. It was incredible. (Connie Pearson)

*   *   *   *

My daughter was my miracle. Also, when I had TB, I was sent to a sanitarium. I was in bed for eight months. They operated and removed my ribs to make my lungs collapse. I had five operations and I prayed to St. Jude. He is my favorite saint. The nuns used to come and pray. I figured by God I am going to get better so I can take care of my daughter. When I walked out of the sanitarium, the doctors were surprised. They thought I would die. (Maryetta Lesniak)

*   *   *   *

Yes, my mother had a massive hemorrhage and should never have lived. Prayer healed her. So I can't deny a miracle. (Esther Miller)

*   *   *   *

My parachute was sabotaged. It was all twisted up when I pulled the ripcord, nothing happened. I began to pull it out and it was all tangled. I was frantically pulling on it. I finally got the lines untwisted. I consider that my closest call. (Phil Miller)

*   *   *   *

Yes, it was just last winter. I had pains and I had to call my sister. I told her that I wasn't able to get out because I wasn't feeling good. I had a heart attack. They got me into the hospital that day and they just made me comfortable. The doctor didn't think I would make it. I did. (Marguerite Balch)

*   *   *   *

My brother said he didn't feel well. The doctor said it was indigestion and told him to go to the veteran's hospital. By this time, he was really feeling badly. They said he had about two months to live. We were going to our cottage up north. I wanted to postpone it but the plan had been made. When we got there during the night, the room got really bright and the sky opened up and there was the most beautiful colors like a rainbow on the lake. I told my husband to look and he didn't see anything. I fell asleep and had a dream. I was in the kitchen with my mother and my aunt who were dead. The doorbell rang and my brother came in all dressed up in a blue suit. I said, "You're well," and gave him a big kiss. That day a man came down to the lake to tell us that my brother had gone into a coma at sunrise and that he had died. When we went to the funeral he was dressed in the same suit as in my dream. (Dorothy Hoskin)

*   *   *   *

The birth of a child is a miracle. We didn't have any children for five years so we wanted to adopt. We got a call from a doctor who was two hundred miles away and told us that the baby we were adopting was born that night. The baby was given to us the next day. So, I thought that was a miracle. (Al Lukeman)

*   *   *   *

Well, life itself is a miracle. The birth of our children and grandchildren were miracles. (Dan Hendriksen)

*   *   *   *

My father, for some reason, was able to heal warts with his hands. He discovered this when he put his hands on this lady's face who had a wart. The next time we saw her, it was gone. He did the same thing for my husband. (Laculia Byrd)

*   *   *   *

I have had so many close calls. I shouldn't be here. So, I guess that it is a miracle that I am still here. (Viola Weber)

*   *   *   *

I have seen that with a lot of sick people. It looked as if they were going to leave this world, but then the good Lord let them stay on. I think that is a miracle. (Ellree Evans)

*   *   *   *

I like to think, particularly in the last few years, that every day is a miracle. (Harold Bulger Jr.)

*   *   *   *

I would call my winnings a miracle. I have been quite lucky. I have won the lottery three times and it was quite a piece of change. That was a miracle for me. (Lillie King Scott)

*   *   *   *

Little bitty ones, you know. I just laugh when these happen and say that my guardian angel keeps awfully busy, little things like that. For example, I was taking some people to a play and the bus was overloaded. The clutch went out and where did it finally stop? It stopped right at the garage that I usually go to. (Elizabeth Purchase)

*   *   *   *

It must have been 1904 or 1905 when I was crippled with infantile paralysis. I had lost the use of my legs. My dad made me a little wheel chair. My grandmother said that she knew an Indian lady. They called her Aunt Sarah and she came and looked me over. She had a bag with some kind of weeds in it. She put them on the ground and took a piece of flint and steel and started a fire. Then when there was smoke, she took her long black and white dress and moved the smoke over my legs. She continued to do that all summer. It was my birthday and Aunt Sarah was there, smoking a pipe. She motioned me to walk over to her. I said that I couldn't get up. She said, "Up, up," and I walked over to her. Later, when I was seventeen, I was able to run the hundred yard dash. I believe I was able to do this because of the faith I had in the Indian woman. Aunt Sarah passed away and the doctor said that she was over one hundred years old when she died. Every Memorial Day I put flowers on her grave. (Ralph Turner)

*   *   *   *

My son was born with Down Syndrome on my twentieth wedding anniversary. My husband's cousin was very religious. She was a good friend of Father Pio and had visited him. She came right over when Todd was born and gave me relics from Father Pio and had him praying for my son. As a youngster growing up, he didn't actually seem to have any handicaps. He has done very well. That is my miracle. (Lois Davis)

*   *   *   *

I really think that finding my husband was sort of a miracle. My mother had died and I was alone. I wanted some support so I prayed to God to send someone that I could marry. It was through a Christmas card that I found my husband. His wife used to send Christmas cards to our family, but in December of 1944, he responded. He told me that he was divorced and we kept writing letters back and forth. He had his mother and boys to take care of, but he came to see me a couple of times and I went to see him during the summer. It was a quick courtship. (Ruth McCaw)

*   *   *   *

I don't know if you can call them true miracles or not. You know, once in a while you think if this hadn't happened it would have been bad news. I can remember when I was in the water in the Aleutian Islands during the war. It was in February and the water was twenty-eight degrees. They had told us that we couldn't survive for more than five minutes and I was in the water for longer than that. All of a sudden, I realized that I could hardly move and yet, somehow I was able to swim to shore. (Jack Streidl)

*   *   *   *

Yes, I was reborn. I saw the Virgin Mary and I gave her water with my hands. I can remember it so vividly. I told my mother and she said I was dreaming. I don't think it was a dream because I had the same clothes on that they wore in the time of Jesus. This experience still sticks in my mind. (Paul Dreer)

CHAPTER 11

▼

Health is the wholeness
of all that we are....
It is the acknowledgment that
our body, mind, and spirit
are one.

What do you do to stay healthy?

I eat healthy food. I learned to eat well on the farm when I was a girl. Even in hard times, we had potatoes, homemade bread, and we churned our own butter. (Maryetta Lesniak)

*   *   *   *

I watch my diet. I walk as much as I can when it is good weather. I like to walk. My church is only a half-block away so I walk there and back. I take medicine for Parkinson's and it keeps it under control. I belong to a support group and they say, "Just keep going, keep going," but it does get me down. (Elaine TenBrink)

*   *   *   *

I don't eat much anymore. But I try to eat a variety of foods and I don't drink. I never have. I don't even know what a drink tastes like. (Gertrude Martin)

*   *   *   *

I grow garlic and use a lot of it. I go very easy on the red meat. I exercise and do a lot of walking. I go get my paper, which is a mile away, and I walk into town which is two and one-half miles. I bale hay, build fences, and make trails in the woods. I am a firm believer in exercise. (Ray Miller)

*   *   *   *

I stay healthy by being optimistic and by doing exercise. (Wu, Xiugang)

*   *   *   *

As a farm kid, I put exercise and health in front of everything else. My exercise is physical work. I also feel that being with a healthy and happy woman keeps me healthy and happy. (Edward Cook Jr.)

*   *   *   *

I exercise in bed before breakfast. I have weights, wrist weights and dumbbells. I have pulmonary thrombosis, emphysema, asthma, and diabetes. I don't take medicine for my diabetes, I just stick with my diet. (Paul Dreer)

*   *   *   *

Well, I'm busy with the boat that I work on. I do have a cleaning lady, but there is always a job ahead of me. I have an apartment building that I attend to. That keeps my mind busy and keeps me occupied. (Al Lukeman)

*   *   *   *

I was brought up to eat a well balanced diet with lots of fruits, vegetables, and protein. I try to do everything for myself that I can. I am on quite a lot of medication now. I am a diabetic, and need to test by blood three times a day when I give myself insulin. I'm now in a wheelchair and have someone living with me to do the things that I can no longer do. I still exercise everyday using weights. (Rosadelle Perry)

*   *   *   *

Well, at my age now, I can't play tennis, jog, or anything like that anymore. Now, I still do physical work. I garden, shovel snow, row my boat, play golf, and fish a lot. I think keeping busy is the main thing. I think that if you just sit around, you will stagnate. So, I keep pretty busy. (Jack Streidl)

*   *   *   *

Well, I was walking every day. I walked better than a mile and when I felt like it, I would go uptown. There was nothing like going out and taking a brisk walk. I can't walk anymore since my fall. I am careful about my food. I have a rather touchy stomach. I don't indulge in fats, sugar, or spicy foods. I try not to over indulge. I don't smoke or drink. (Lydia Nickerson)

*   *   *   *

I am confident to live over one hundred. I have sickness, problems in the heart, gallbladder, and also bone connections. I am still very confident and encouraged that I will fight disease and live a long live. I have a very positive attitude and I do exercise. (Geng Zheng)

*   *   *   *

I have cholesterol problems so I walk. I also try to watch my diet. I try to keep on reading. I did some writing and I do crossword puzzles for my mental health. Sometimes getting in a dialogue with people who like to talk about issues and even perhaps argue the issues keeps me mentally challenged. (Dan Hendriksen)

*   *   *   *

I like to keep busy. I like to work outdoors. I eat what I want to eat. I don't stick to any certain foods. If I want dessert, I eat dessert. If I give my horse a carrot, I eat one to. I eat meat, potatoes, and vegetables. (Viola Weber)

*   *   *   *

I thank goodness that I was born with good genes. I keep myself very active and I exercise. I walk everyday. I don't worry about my diet. I eat everything. Luckily I don't have a craving for sweets. I crave salads. I don't eat in abundance and if something doesn't agree with me, I don't eat it. If I gain a couple of pounds then I eat less starch. (Lois Davis)

*   *   *   *

My wife and I have many ailments that crowd our lives. We try to live around them. We pursue an exercise routine such as swimming daily, drink wine in moderation, establish a healthy diet, take vacations, and use our energies to pursue activities that use our skills. (George Vargish)

*   *   *   *

Well, I walk a lot to keep busy. You see when I was a child, I couldn't sit around the house like some kids do today. I learned to stay active. (Ellree Evans)

*   *   *   *

Well, I picked the right genes. My dad lived to be ninety-seven and my mother was ninety-five when she died. I don't smoke and I didn't abuse alcohol. I don't say that I never had a glass of wine for dinner because I did. If it was okay for Jesus, I guess it is okay for me. (Elizabeth Purchase)

*   *   *   *

I have always tried to teach my students to eat well, sleep well, pray well, and play well. So, that is what I do. (Alba "Polly" Pollard)

*   *   *   *

I just walk a little bit and do work in the garden in the summer time. I watch my diet. (Marguerite Balch)

*   *   *   *

I walk more than an hour everyday. I eat whatever I want. (Florence Atkins)

*   *   *   *

I take ginger root, vitamins A and C. I learned in school to keep a balance by eating a mixture of foods to stay healthy. I am not a very heavy meat eater. (Esther Miller)

*   *   *   *

I think we eat well. Jack gets a great deal of exercise. My exercise is confined to housework. We have been lucky. We have good doctors and haven't let things go. (Phyllis Streidl)

*   *   *   *

I work out three times a week. I warm up for fifteen minutes on the treadmill or bicycle and then do nautilus for forty-five minutes. I also take tap dancing one day a week for an hour. I have gotten where I don't like meat very much anymore. I just use it to flavor noodles. I insist on butter, but it is the light whipped. (Beth Sambo)

*   *   *   *

I eat well. I don't drink a lot. (Robert Applegate)

*   *   *   *

I have always eaten well. I eat a lot of fruits and vegetables. I walk for exercise. (Dorothy Hoskin)

*   *   *   *

I don't think that I am doing too bad for my age. I try to watch my diet because I had open heart surgery back in 1983, but I haven't had any trouble since. I do a lot of reading, thinking, and watching television for my mental health. (Gordon French)

*   *   *   *

I split wood, I play tennis, badminton, and basketball. I try to do something everyday to get tired physically. Beef, pork, and milk are things that I don't eat anymore. (Richard Tanner)

*   *   *   *

I take my vitamins and try to do things for myself. I went to California, Florida, and Toronto. I think traveling is good for my health. (Ethel Cutshall)

*   *   *   *

I listen to music. I love the harp. Music keeps me healthy. (Gertrude Powell)

CHAPTER 12

▼

Memories are our life experiences....
They can hold us in the past
or be the bridge that supports
and comforts us
in the present.

What is your most vivid memory?

The most important memory in my life is not so much an isolated incident, but the influence of the older people in my family. My grandfather was a very religious man and probably the most important influence, not only for myself, but on all the grandchildren in the family. I always felt that it was up to me to live up to the reputation that he and the older members of the family had established in whatever community we lived. I was fortunate to have known my great grandparents and their brothers and sisters. I used to enjoy listening to them talk about all the things that happened in their lifetime. (Rosadelle Perry)

*   *   *   *

My mother would never let me have a dog in the house. She was a strict housekeeper. I had always wanted a dog and that particular Christmas, I went down the basement and there was a toboggan. That's what I was going to get for Christmas. My dad went downstairs to get my present and he came upstairs with a real Fox Terrier in a box. Wow, I started to cry, my mom was crying, my dad was crying, and my friends were crying. We all stood there while I held that little dog. (Robert Applegate)

*   *   *   *

What I remember most is going to college from 1936 to 1940. I went to the University of Maine. I remember the general atmosphere. It was a happy go lucky era. There seemed to be no problems. Also, I had a pretty good record in football. I made All State and All New England. I was probably the first one in New England to wear a face mask. (Edward Cook Jr.)

*   *   *   *

Every season and every occurrence brings memories. I am in my late seventies and I have lots of memories. Life and death, marriages, that kind of thing, they surface from time to time. The biggest, of course, was my husband Jack going in the Navy. The second time was when he went off for the Korean War. We had four children and I was pregnant with my fifth when he left. (Phyllis Streidl)

*   *   *   *

It's hard to say, the school years, being married, and building a house near Lake Michigan in 1959 was a big thrill. The hardest part was when my husband had a heart attack. He was only forty-one years old when he had his first coronary and he recovered very well from that. Then he had a second massive coronary and from then on he was a semi-invalid. I had to work. I worked twenty-five years as a secretary for an accounting firm. I was really fortunate to have the work. I was respected and appreciated. That really makes a difference when people appreciate what you are doing. (Esther Miller)

*   *   *   *

My most vivid memory was coming home when I was a child to the smell of homemade bread. I also remember my mother churning the butter. All the kids would help. (Maryetta Lesniak)

*   *   *   *

I grew up in the depression and anything we did was a plus. My wife and I were married at eighteen and nineteen with no money at all. We went to Indiana to get married and we didn't even have any money for the preacher. We were married for sixty-three years. (Robert Van Blarcom)

*   *   *   *

I have so many memories. I have so many happy memories and I have sad memories. I think the one that stands out is the day that my husband and I celebrated 50 years of marriage. I stood on the beach with him that day and cried. It was a wonderful feeling because both of our kids and their spouses were with us. (Patricia Henry)

*   *   *   *

I am sure that we all have things that happen. I remember one time, Jack my brother and I had separate beds but we shared a bedroom. He had appendicitis and was moaning and groaning and the doctor was in the house. All I did was lay there cowering, thinking what is going to happen. He did get better. (Tyrus Fouchey)

*   *   *   *

I remember the time I had the measles and I couldn't play with my brother. He was sitting on one side of the door frame and I was sitting on the other. I also remember when I was in the school choir but I wasn't supposed to sing, only move my lips because my voice was so bad. Then when Ty and I got married, times were very difficult. We found a small flat, there was very little housing. We couldn't buy a refrigerator or a car for awhile because the manufacturing companies were making things for the war. (Millicent Fouchey)

*   *   *   *

I remember taking a train to Detroit, Michigan when I was nine years old. My mother and father and the younger children were on the train. I watched the towns, farms, landscape, and life outside. That was in 1921. We spent the night on the train and slept in berths and that was very exciting. (Dorothy Hoskin)

*   *   *   *

I worked at General Motors for twenty-five years and I retired when I was fifty-eight years old. My husband and I decided that it was time that we did something that we liked. We went to the Bahamas, Jamaica, and eleven countries in Europe. It was something that we wanted to do before we were too old to enjoy it. (Laculia Byrd)

*   *   *   *

I can remember the day I was married and the day my first child was born. I remember being a prisoner of war for thirteen months. I remember being in a disabled airplane and seeing them waiting for me on the ground and me thinking, "I will not live out this day." (Phil Miller)

*   *   *   *

Getting married and having a family was an exciting time and it is a vivid memory. I guess when I was in the service, I had something happen that was most interesting. When I was coming in for a landing and the airplane cut out and it took me a minute or two to figure out what was going on. I switched to another tank and it took off again. For a few minutes that was kind of memorable. When I was in New Zealand two years ago, I went with a youth group to the national forest in the south of New Zealand. I decided to do para-sailing off a mountain. I was strapped to the man who had the parachute. It was beautiful. (Richard Tanner)

*   *   *   *

I survived a hurricane on Nevis. Roofs and houses were down. They took all the children and went to the church. I stayed in the house. I wasn't afraid but I couldn't sleep. I had a flashlight. The water was beating on the windows but I still wouldn't leave the house. (Lorita Powell)

*   *   *   *

I served my country during World War II at Guatemala Canal. I had the experience of seeing the ship that we were on hit by the Japanese. We lost most of our company and the entire ship. I will never forget that. (Gordon TenBrink)

*   *   *   *

When the depression hit we lived on a farm. I was ten years old. We were such a big family, all my brothers and sisters. My father had to sell the car and ride a horse and buggy. We realized that was all my father could do, but all the kids were so embarrassed. We were very poor, we weren't alone, and everyone was poor. Those are the kind of things I remember. It was rough. Now that I look back, I realize that we were the rich ones. My dad taught us not to feel sorry for ourselves. (Evelyn Moore)

*   *   *   *

Adopting our children was enormously exciting. You never know when you adopt what to expect. The boy was the first child and the girl, the second. (Elaine TenBrink)

*   *   *   *

My most vivid memory was when I was married. I was seventeen and my husband was almost eighteen years old, so I was married early. My husband carried the mail for forty-one years. Everyone loved him. He was a friend to everyone on his route. (Gertrude Martin)

*   *   *   *

After 86 years, it is very difficult to select one event. Probably the most vivid memories were when I married my wife Emmaline more than 60 years ago and the birth of my daughter, Nancy. (George Vargish)

*   *   *   *

I remember my childhood. I was called "Dutch Cleaner" because I always wanted to clean. My brother would want to know why I was vacuuming when everyone else was trying to sleep. I didn't have that thought. I was awake and I was getting the house clean. I also remember sitting on the porch talking and reading. I was always speaking with people, saying hello and good morning when they would go to work. Even as a child, I was always reaching out, reaching out. (Alba "Polly" Pollard)

*   *   *   *

When I was a little boy of about four years old, I was jumping on the bed. At that time, they had iron bars at the end. I landed on one of the bars and the blood spurted out and I was rushed to the hospital. The doctors stitched me without giving me any kind of anesthetic. I can still remember screaming bloody murder.

I still have the scar. So, that is a vivid memory even though it was a long time ago. (Dan Hendriksen)

*   *   *   *

I still remember and miss the life in the country when I was young and a farmer. When I planted I just felt happy and the air was so fresh. I don't like city life. It is too crowded. Here the people deal with people, not with nature. (Wu, Xiugang)

*   *   *   *

My most impressive memories were life when I was a teacher. I taught very young children. I have professional training for early education. The children always accepted the beauty, the good things. They were able to take big advantage of what I taught them. (Geng, Zheng)

*   *   *   *

Well, when I was a kid on the farm, we always raised turkeys. We would have a turkey raffle in the fall. The turkeys would go after the grasshoppers and be way over in the neighbor's woods. It was my job to bring them back. We would put numbers on them with a string around their back and we would put them all in the pen. We would have the raffle by having everyone throw the dice. When they won, I would get the turkey for them. (Viola Weber)

*   *   *   *

I remember a lot of things. I remember when I was working on the farm. It was a beautiful life. It was freedom. The farm was in Mississippi. (Florence Atkins)

*   *   *   *

My mother had twelve children. We all worked on the farm and worked outdoors all summer. We would drive the team of horses to plow the fields. We had to clean the barn and pick cucumbers. My dad would take them to Kalamazoo to sell. (Marguerite Balch)

CHAPTER 13

▼

When we connect spiritually
with a higher power, it can change our lives....
We are comforted in knowing
that we are never alone.

What does spirituality mean in your life?

I believe spirituality is very important. I've really always denied it—I came out of the war feeling that I didn't believe in God. I found that I was feeling empty and was trying to find something. That is how I became a Quaker. I found it was really what I wanted. I believe in people who are trying to solve their problems and living their life the best they can. (Robert Applegate)

*   *   *   *

I think religion is very important. It is vital and I don't know what I would do without it. I am not a member of any church, but I support whatever church I happen to be going to. I think the main thing is that we don't need to go through someone to get a hearing with God. I think we each have a direct line and ought to be using it. (Robert Tanner)

*   *   *   *

You have to believe in something. I'm not as spiritual as many. I do belong to the Methodist church. I think religion and spirituality are one in the same. The church teaches kids what they need to know and it teaches wisdom. My son teaches Sunday school. (Phil Miller)

*   *   *   *

I believe in life after death. I am not a church going person, but I believe that God has made the beauty of the world. (Patricia Henry)

*   *   *   *

It is important to me. I pray every day. (Christina Hudson)

*   *   *   *

Religion is very important in my family life. I pray everyday. I pray for my family all the time and I go to church regularly. I do things when I can for others. (Millicent Fouchey)

*   *   *   *

I was born and raised a Catholic and went to Catholic school for twelve years. Religion is part of my life. (Tyrus Fouchey)

*   *   *   *

Religion is very important. It is a very big part of my life. It is not something I talk about but I have been active in one church or another. It is always in the back of everything. You talk about who your role models are, Christ is mine. I always want to be a good person. I guess that is what I rely on for strength. I really do. I mean I don't sit and read passages from the Bible or anything. Silently, I pray daily. (Beth Sambo)

*   *   *   *

Well, I think being religious helps. You know if things get to where you can't do anything about them, you can always turn to prayer and hope that will carry you over. We go to church on Sunday and Phyllis is in study. We both are involved in adoration one hour a week. (Jack Streidl)

*   *   *   *

Religion is important to me, especially in the last year. I just went through an operation and it was more serious than I thought. It took me a long time to recover. I had so much help from my church and from the people in the church. I think I got about sixty letters from them. They were really wonderful to me. I never was lonely even though I was in the hospital for two weeks and in a nursing home for two weeks. (Dorothy Hoskin)

*   *   *   *

I definitely believe in God and I believe in prayer. I think prayer is very important and during my husband's illness and when the children were ill, it gave me satisfaction to be able to pray. (Lois Davis)

*   *   *   *

Spirituality is very important. I'm not a church goer as I used to be. I am always saying prayers throughout the day. It is always on my mind. (Evelyn Moore)

*   *   *   *

We were all church people. We went to church and Sunday school. I have great respect for religion. (Marjorie Pierce)

*   *   *   *

I have my devotions every morning. I write my prayers and I write down in my journal what I have done the day before. I do my reading, praying, and asking for guidance. (Esther Miller)

*   *   *   *

Now that I have time, I spend Tuesday morning at church for Holy Hour, study, and mass. Tuesday morning, I feel like I have covered all the bases. (Phyllis Streidl)

*   *   *   *

We were quite religious in the early years and not as much in the adult years. I am a firm believer that it is not how deep you are in the religious community, but how you conduct yourself each day. (Edward Cook Jr.)

* * * *

I pray quite a bit and went to church for years. I pray every night and at every meal. (Ralph Turner)

* * * *

Yes, I am a Catholic. I do a lot of praying when things go bad and I do believe that prayers help. (Viola Weber)

* * * *

Well you know, I'm not all that active in the church but I depend on God to help me. I do a lot of praying and someone is always saying, "I want you to pray for me because I know your prayers go through." (Laculia Byrd)

* * * *

Spirituality is very important to me. It has helped me many times. You pray for other people to help them. That is what I do. (Ethel Cutshall)

* * * *

I think that religion is good and that you need it. Religion answers a great many questions that people have. It helps solve problems. You can always turn to God. (Gordon French)

* * * *

Spirituality has always been important in my life. I started attending church before I can even remember anything else. The first church meetings were held in my grandfather's home. That was before the congregation was wealthy enough to build a church. Spirituality still plays an important role in my life. (Rosadelle Perry)

*   *   *   *

Religion is very important. It is my life line. I have been a Catholic since the day I was born. To know or to realize, and to accept the fact that there is someone up there bigger than I am, has helped me through a lot of life's ups and downs. I just feel a sense of peace when I can go to mass on Sunday. (Connie Pearson)

*   *   *   *

Spirituality is very important. Without the love of God, Jesus, and the Holy Spirit, I don't think that I would be here today. He's been my guide throughout my life. (Ruth McCaw)

*   *   *   *

Oh, it's real important to me. I was baptized when I was fifteen years old. I got aquatinted with the Lord in 1937. I'll never forget that. I thank Jesus for every day that he lets me live. When I get up in the morning I put one foot in front of the other, I say," Thank you Jesus for letting me see another day." I walk out on my porch, when I get out there I say," Thank you God." I look up and see His darling sun. He rules from high in the East and He is making His way on across to the West. I thank God for that. (Ellree Evans)

*   *   *   *

Well, I enjoy going to church. I believe in the Lord, definitely. I have many, many beautiful friends at different churches. (Gertrude Martin)

*   *   *   *

I have been around religion all my life. It has never meant as much to me as it does since I moved here. I am alone and I listen to Sunday church programs on television. I pray at night when I go to bed. (Hilda Wesseling)

*   *   *   *

My personal conviction is that faith in God is the greatest power to see us through the challenge of living. But we have to work at solving our problems. (George Vargish)

*   *   *   *

Religion is not important to me. But, I can understand why it is important to other people. Religion can do a lot of good. However, the way religions clash with each other certainly creates a lot of problems in the world. (Ray Miller)

*   *   *   *

Religion is important, but I don't go to church. You don't have to go to church to believe in God. (Paul Dreer)

*   *   *   *

Religion is my life. It is my life. I truly love the Lord and my life depends on him. I know that I couldn't have made it as far as this if he hadn't been in my life. He means everything to me. He has opened so many doors. Anytime I undertook anything, I asked him to guide me. People sometimes say to me, "You think you are something." I say, "I know I am something, I am a child of God." (Lillie King Scott)

*   *   *   *

It is the most important thing in my life. I feel that religion is not like a cloak that you can put on and take off one day a week or on Sunday. Everyday is a new day and the first day of the rest of your life. Therefore, you try to live it to the fullest. If I want to be like Christ, I'm supposed to seek Christ in you, Christ in every other person. I can't do that if Christ is not living within me. Although I am a Catholic, I am a Christian first. In the end, God isn't going to ask you whether you were a good Catholic, Baptist, or Methodist. He is going to ask how you chose to take care of your fellow man. (Alba "Polly" Pollard)

*   *   *   *

Yes, to a great extent. I was brought up in the Christian church, and I have always gone. I look forward to it. (Lydia Nickerson)

*   *   *   *

If religion wasn't important I wouldn't have it. I am a church going woman. I was raised up on religion. I don't have to have any special time to pray, I can walk around and pray. I live a good, blessed life. I am just with the will of the Lord, that is all. I thank God for that. (Florence Atkins)

*   *   *   *

Spirituality is very important. I even write about it at the present time. I grade lessons for prisoners and their lessons are in fact, around religious themes. I then write them letters of encouragement. I also write a monthly article for a church paper under the heading "Out of the Mouth of Babies and Olders". I enjoy that. (Dan Hendriksen)

*   *   *   *

I think it's important, not to loudly profess it, but to do things that I believe in. I get inward satisfaction when I am working with people. I think that is what I am supposed to do. (Harold Bulger Sr.)

*   *   *   *

To a certain extent I think spirituality is important. I go to church. I go to the Methodist church because it is close. (Marguerite Balch)

*   *   *   *

Well, I always went to church but now that I am 105, I have to have the church come to me. A lot of my friends from church visit me. (Gertrude Powell)

*   *   *   *

It is very important. I don't always understand it. It is the sort of thing that you can't put into words. I have gone to a lot of workshops on spirituality. It is really what religion is. It is the spirit. It gives me courage. I was involved in a group named by Eric Crow called the Bethlehem Group because this translated to the "house of bread". So we made bread and meals. It wasn't free but it was inexpensive. I now go to a Presbyterian Church and our pastor is Reverend Cunningham. (Elizabeth Purchase)

*   *   *   *

I am not a daily mass goer but I have been very close to my church since I was a young boy. I was an alter boy and never had a desire to be a priest. As a young boy growing up, I had young brothers and sisters. I would put a sheet around me and say daily mass and they would follow me. We would perform these rituals a couple times a week on a soap box that we used as an alter. Since then, I have faithfully gone to mass on Sundays and followed my religion but respected everyone else's. (Al Lukeman)

CHAPTER 14

▼

Marriage is a commitment
of two souls....
Together they love, honor, respect,
and share their lives.

What do you think makes a successful marriage?

I never knew anyone who worked harder than my wife. When I bought my insurance agency in 1951, she worked for me when my secretary quit. Then we bought a house and built an office in it. She did all the office work, all the housework, and took care of the kids. She worked hard and I worked hard too. We supported each other. (Phil Miller)

*   *   *   *

We have been together for so long that we just get along, that is all there is to it. When I broke my leg, he took care of me. When he is sick, I take care of him. (Patricia Henry)

*   *   *   *

Well, in the first place you can't just think of yourself. You have to be a little bit unselfish. If you can't you're going to have a lot of problems. You are going to argue. We had a lot of dandy's, but when you go to bed you have to forget about them and start a new day tomorrow. (Robert Van Blarcom)

*   *   *   *

Look at the bright side and trust in the Lord that everything will come out all right. I did. We were married for seventy years. Verna and I never had an argument. She was a wonderful girl. We went through things together and did things together. (Ralph Turner)

*   *   *   *

You need to understand one another and to be honest and faithful. (Dorothy Hoskin)

*   *   *   *

I was married for fifty-two years. When I first met my husband, my friend introduced me to him. My friend knew that we would end up together. He was a good lover. We went on dates, shows, and dances. There was always music. (Maryetta Lesniak)

*   *   *   *

We were married in 1933. Nine months and two weeks later we had our first baby. Thirteen months later we had another one and then we had our third. He was a good father. We supported each other naturally. He was just a wonderful man. (Esther Miller)

*   *   *   *

I think we were very supportive of one another. He was a great father. (Lois Davis)

*   *   *   *

Love each other and listen to each other. Depend on each other to overcome problems. Even when my wife had cancer, she was the same women she always was. We turned to each other for guidance and strength. (Robert Applegate)

*   *   *   *

He was working every day. I stayed home to begin with and took care of the kids. We had one after another, six of them in twelve years. We struggled and we made it. (Christina Hudson)

*   *   *   *

A successful marriage depends on how happy you are and how happy the other person is. You have to be able to bend a little. (Gordon French)

*   *   *   *

You have to give and take and help one another out when they need it. Each of you have different ideas about some things and you have to come to an understanding by working and talking things out. That is what married life is all about. It is about giving and taking. Everybody has problems. Things aren't going to work out perfect all the time. As a matter of fact, I think it would be kind of dull if it did. (Ethel Cutshall)

*   *   *   *

Neither one of us completely dominated the marriage. I won't say that there weren't disagreements but in most cases we reached a compromise that met the requirements of each of us. We gave each other a little space. (Rosadelle Perry)

*   *   *   *

I hate to say acceptance yet that is what it is. I could say being tolerant. We don't try to change each other. We accept each other. (Harold Bulger Jr.)

*   *   *   *

To support him, I worked so that it would help. I tried to support him and his family. (Elaine TenBrink)

*   *   *   *

The reason we have a successful marriage is that we always pulled together. We were a team. We celebrated our fiftieth wedding anniversary. It was such a tremendous event. We had so many people that we had the activity in our church. We were so grateful for those years God had given us together. We had the opportunity not only to support ourselves, but to contribute to the people around us that were going through hardships. (Gordon TenBrink)

*   *   *   *

I do the so called "woman things" and he does the so called "man things". That is the way he wants it. He is very traditional in that sense. (Beth Sambo)

*   *   *   *

Give into each other. Give a little, take a little. Marriage is a fifty-fifty proposition. We have had about three arguments in all the time we have been together. When I met her, I knew that I had found the woman that I loved and was going to marry. I have been happy ever since. (Paul Dreer)

*   *   *   *

We have been married over fifty-seven years. We never had any conflicts that amounted to anything in all those years. You know, we might have disagreed a little bit on something or another, but we worked it out. If Phyllis' knees are bothering her, then I do the floors and wash the dishes. I had a hip replaced and I couldn't do much, she waited on me. That is what marriage is all about. (Jack Streidl)

*   *   *   *

One can't be the boss. You have to work together. I think they should definitely work together. I don't think it hurts a man one bit to wipe dishes once in awhile. I think a husband and wife should share the responsibilities. (Hilda Wesseling)

*   *   *   *

I had a successful marriage because we both tried to do the best we could with our lives. We were both church members, which helped. We were both happy and content and worked hard for what we got. Also, I have to say that my husband was very easy to live with and that makes all the difference in the world. He wasn't looking for trouble or anything. We both tried to do our own work and carry our own load. (Lydia Nickerson)

*   *   *   *

Well, my husband teased that I robbed the cradle because he is one year younger than I am. We always said the we would rather fight than switch. One thing I told my husband was never go to bed mad because you might not wake up. So, I think he always thought about that because we never did. (Laculia Byrd)

*   *   *   *

Understand that you have to talk things out. You have to ask, "What do you think about this or that?" Let each other be their own person. (Lillie King Scott)

*   *   *   *

Marriage means to live loving each other. A good wife is one who listens to her husband and stays by his side. (Lorita Powell)

*   *   *   *

I think you have to use humor once in awhile. Also don't take yourself too seriously. Our religious beliefs suggest that we try to work things out and not just part ways when you disagree. We have done that. We have good times together and enjoy each other. We also have a good relationship with our family and extended family. (Dan Hendriksen)

*   *   *   *

I think that a lot of luck is involved. When people are choosing a mate they can overlook some flaws in their intended. Then, they have to think about whether they would want children with those qualities. Often the parent's qualities show up in the children. (Phyllis Streidl)

*   *   *   *

I think we were an inspiration to each other and we talked things over. If the boys wanted to do anything, it wasn't the case of go ask mom, go ask dad. We would have a little consultation together before giving an answer. (Ruth McCaw)

CONCLUSION

▼

As my sister and I get ready to publish this book, it is hard to imagine that our journey began almost a decade ago. At that time, my hobby was genealogy and I was involved in searching for information on my ancestors. Although, I was able to locate documentation on my grandparents, great grandparents, and great, great grandparents, I realized how little I knew about the lives of my mother and dad. By then, both of them had died. I regretted the fact that I had not taken the time to sit down and talk to them about their past.

Since my sister, Loretta, had extensive experience working with seniors, I went to see her. After talking, we decided to collaborate on a project that would honor seniors and document their thoughts, ideas, and perceptions. Together, we hoped that we would be able to share their experiences, offer inspirational reading for others, and provide families with written documentation about the lives of their loved ones. Through this process, we were able to develop and co-author our first book, *Hearts of Seniors*.

As this project comes to an end, we look back on this memorable experience. It afforded us with hours of interesting conversation with diverse men and women. It opened our eyes to the courage that it takes to face the struggles that come with aging and the importance of taking time to celebrate each day. This endeavor has changed our lives forever.

Many of the men and women we interviewed have since passed on. Although Ralph Turner died in 1999, we will never forget the loving way he spoke about his beloved wife, Verna. Dorothy Hoskin died as she had always lived, loving her family and trusting in God. Although Phil Miller passed away, we will remember his generous spirit and giving nature. He shared his network of family and friends with us by opening the door to others whom we were able to interview. In memory of Marjorie Pierce, a college scholarship fund for young people in the Shrewsbury area was set up. Tyrus Fouchey, our brother-in-law, lost his courageous battle with Leukemia. He was an honorable man whose life revolved around his wife and family.

To those seniors who have gone before us and to those who are with us today, we are truly grateful for this experience. In different ways, each of the interviews has had an impact on how we look at this formidable generation. We are honored to share this book with the men and women we interviewed, their families, and others who are interested in the lives of seniors.

In the back of the book, we have provided a place for families to put a picture and a biography of their loved one. The questions that follow give you an opportunity to sit down with your parent, grandparent, relative, or friend and find out more about his or her life. When you document this information, this book will then become a family treasure that can be passed on from generation to generation.

PICTURES AND BIOGRAPHIES

▼

Bob Applegate was born in Detroit, Michigan in1921. He served in World War II. Because of his experiences in the war he became a pacifist. Following those beliefs, Bob joined the Quakers. He began his career in journalism by writing for the school newspaper at Michigan State University. After graduation, he was married and had four children. He started working for the Free Press  and later became a reporter for the Adrian Newspaper. When Bob retired, he continued to be involved in freelance writing. He enjoyed his grandchildren, dog and cat, gardening in the spring, thinking, and photography.

 Florence Atkins was born on July 3, 1916. She was raised on a farm in Mississippi. She came from a large family and had sixteen brothers and sisters. Florence survived the loss of two husbands and is grateful for her daughter who was always there for her. Working has been an integral part of her life. She volunteered at the senior center helping to provide meals. Florence was always a very spiritual person who enjoyed walking and praying in the late afternoon. She felt that her life has been blessed and directed by God.

Marguerite Balch was born on a farm on August 18, 1908. As one of twelve children, she had to help raise her brothers and sisters. She also worked on the farm driving the team of horses, plowing the fields, cleaning the barn, and picking cucumbers. She graduated from high school in 1925 and attended college. She left school to work at the state hospital to take care of patients. She married and raised eight children and all of them are successful. Marguerite was a widow who enjoyed shuffle board, playing cards, traveling, tending to her flower garden, and being involved in politics by working at the polls during elections.

Laculia Byrd was born on February 10, 1910 and grew up in Mayfield, Kentucky. Her father had been a slave and ran away at the age of 14 to join the Army. Laculia was able to go to college during the depression since her father received a pension for being a civil war vet. She graduated from college in 1933 and taught in a country school. She was married in 1935 and came to Pontiac, Michigan. Although she tried to get a teaching job, she was turned down because of her color. Laculia then worked at General Motors and retired after 25 years. After raising her family, she traveled the world.

Harold Bulger was born in Chicago on May 19, 1923. He graduated from high school and enlisted in the Navy in 1942. After leaving the service, he was married. A year later he re-enlisted and stayed in the service until his last tour of Vietnam twenty-one years later. He then began working in the private sector and his last position was with the Department of Labor with the State

of Michigan. Harold has volunteered for Habitat for Humanities, NSHA, and the NAACP. Harold is most proud of his son and daughter-in-law.

Ed Cook Jr. was born on a Vermont dairy farm in January of 1917. He graduated from the University of Maine with a degree in agriculture and an outstanding record in football. He was All State and All New England. In 1940 Ed found a job in Woodstock at the County Extension Services and met his wife. He joined the Air Force in 1942. Upon discharge he became an agricultural instructor and eventually started his own landscaping business. Ed has been a tax collector in Shrewsbury, Vermont for over twenty years. He raised two daughters and has five grandchildren.

Ethel Cutshall was born in Cleve-
land, Ohio on September 25, 1911.
She was married in 1933 and had a
son and daughter. Ethel completed
high school at Jane Addams Technical School where she learned the
skills that she used many years later
to care for her mother. Ethel was
proud of her husband who worked at
his son's business five days a week at
the age of ninety-three. She enjoyed
helping others, spending time with

her children, grand children, and great grandchildren. Ethel was content sitting
in her garden with her cherished cats.

Lois Davis was born into a loving home in
Toledo, Ohio. She went to a Catholic girl's
school and then to the University of Toledo
where she received a degree in business. She
was hired by IBM in system services and
worked as a salesperson for a period of time.
She married in 1948 and had eight children.
Lois is now a widow and lives with her
youngest son Todd who has special needs and
is an accomplished athlete. Lois has wonderful friends, takes trips each year visiting her
children in foreign countries, and does volunteer work. She says the only thing that would
make her happier would be to improve her
golf game.

Paul Dreer was born in Hamtramck, Michigan on June 14, 1926. He was the middle child in a family of three. He contracted polio when he was a boy and suffered a deformity of his one foot. He was determined, however, at a young age not to let his handicap interfere with his life. He left home at sixteen to see the country and learned self-reliance. Eventually, Paul returned home to marry and start a family. He was hired at a

linen company and worked there until he retired thirty years later. He enjoyed the company of his wonderful wife, children, grandchildren and the family reunions each summer.

Ellree Evans was born on July 5, 1922. She enjoyed going to school with her sixteen sisters and brothers. Ellree was married in 1945 and had a family. Her husband passed away in 1980. She worked in a nursing home for many years until her retirement in 1986. She volunteered at the Ecumenical Center for seniors five days a week. She was an avid walker and participated in many walkathons. Religion was always a very important part of Ellree's life. She was satisfied at the end of the day when she knew

the good Lord would say "Well done." She said talking and laughing with good people made her happy.

Millicent Fouchey was born in Detroit, Michigan on June 28, 1925. She was the oldest child and had three sisters and one brother. She married Tyrus Fouchey in 1946 and they had six children. When her youngest daughter was in high school, Millicent became a Para professional and worked with severely emotionally impaired children. She retired eleven years later. In her spare time, she was an avid reader. Today,  she enjoys her children, grandchildren, great grandchildren, and family. Millicent has kept close contact with her friends from elementary school and continues to enjoy time out with the "girls."

 Tyrus Fouchey was born on February 11, 1921 in Detroit, Michigan. He was one of four boys in a close knit family. The boys spent their free time fishing in the Detroit River. He graduated from high school in 1939. In 1946 he married Millicent Garner and later raised a family of six children. He worked as an electrician and retired in 1983. Tyrus' favorite activities were the opera, fishing, bowling, and playing cards. He and Millicent celebrated their fiftieth wedding anniversary with family and friends in 1996. He enjoyed living a quiet life and spending quality time with his family.

Gordon French was born the oldest of five children on September 25, 1922. He received a Master's Degree in chemistry at the University of Michigan. While teaching at Western Michigan University, he accepted a position at the Upjohn Pharmaceutical Company where he was employed for thirty-six years.  Gordon was married and had four children and one grandchild. Besides working part-time, Gordon volunteered for the AARP helping seniors complete their income tax returns. Gordon says that his greatest reward is giving back to the community that has given so much to him.

 Dan Hendricksen was born in 1929. He finished both high school and college in Grand Rapids, Michigan. He was drafted in the Army during the Korean War and was sent overseas. Dan met Shirley at the elementary school where they were both teaching and married her in 1954. He left teaching and returned to college to receive his Ph.D. in linguistics. He then taught at Western University and retired after 26 years. After retirement, Dan and Shirley went to Russia to teach English. He continues to travel with his wife, enjoy his children and grandchildren while working part-time.

Patricia Henry was the oldest of eight children and was born on June 27, 1928 in Kalamazoo, Michigan. She represented one of the five generations of her family at the time of the interview. Pat, a retired bookkeeper has a mathematical mind. Recently, Pat and her husband celebrated their fiftieth wedding anniversary with their family on an Island off the coast of Venezuela. Presently, her family is building a cabin in Northern Michigan. She enjoys gardening, wall papering, making cakes for friends, and working on local and national elections. Pat has just published a book entitled "The History of Oakwood, a Community of Kalamazoo, Michigan."

Dorothy Hoskin was born on October 4, 1912 in Mohawk, Michigan. She came from a large family and was one of ten children. Her family moved from the Upper Peninsula when Dorothy was young. Here she met her future husband and was married when she was twenty-one years old. She stayed home and raised her daughter and two sons. When her children were older, Dorothy started volunteer work in the hospital and convalescent home. After she lost her beloved husband Don, she became a grief counselor for other men and women who had lost their spouse. Dorothy most enjoyed the company of family and friends.

Christina Hudson was born into a large family on October 12, 1911. She had ten brothers and sisters and learned at an early age the importance of caring for one another. She was married in 1935 and had six children in twelve years. Christina was a stay at home mother who cared for her family. She is a devote Catholic, whose religious beliefs helped substance her after the deaths of her husband and daughter. Later, she moved into a senior citizen complex where she made many friends. Christina has a very close family and enjoys spending time with her children, grand-children, and great grandchildren.

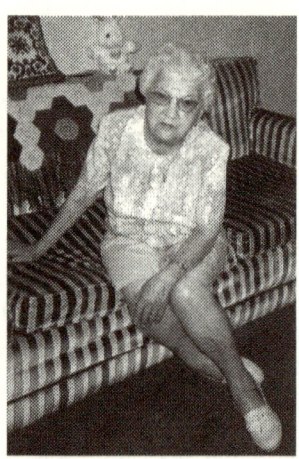

Maryetta Lesniak was born on June 4, 1915 to immigrant parents who came over from Belgium and eventu-ally settled in Bay City, Michigan. She was one of eight children and was raised on a farm. Maryetta mar-ried and later moved to Texas with her daughter and her husband who was in the service. While working in a factory, she contracted tuberculosis and was sent to a sanitarium for eight months. Miraculously, she recovered and the family moved back to Michigan. She lived with her daughter and son-in-law in El Paso, Texas for many years. She enjoyed spending time with her grandchildren and great grandchildren.

Al Lukeman was born on a farm in Franklin, Illinois on June 17, 1913. After graduating from high school in 1931, Al hitchhiked to Chillicothe College in Missouri, where he worked as a security guard for tuition. He enlisted in the Navy and served at Guadalcanal. Returning home, he worked for Esquire magazine in promotion and advertising. Sixteen years later, he was offered a position with Doubleday and became the top sales person of the year. Al's first wife died leaving him with three children. Al remarried and had a son. Al is passionate about life. He loves beautiful women, friends of all ages, and children.

No photo available

Ruth McCraw was born in upstate New York in September of 1907. When Ruth grew up, she became a teacher following in the footsteps of her mother. After a whirlwind courtship, she married her old school friend with two children in 1925. Ruth continued teaching after her husband died of cancer and started volunteering at the Hospice center. Eventually, she moved to Kalamazoo to be closer to her son who is a Methodist Minister. Ruth continued her volunteer work and made quilts, bibs, and caps for babies. She also worked in the health center cheering up patients. Ruth had a happy, fulfilling life.

Gertrude Martin was born on July 18, 1899 on a farm in Climax, Michigan. She received her schooling in a one room school house. She was married to her husband in 1917 and had two daughters, all of whom have since passed away. She was thankful for her grandchildren, great grandchildren, and family. Gertrude talked about her joy of collecting antiques, painting china, sewing, and dancing. She belonged to a study group that was involved in many activities including quilt making. Although she was limited physically, she continued to enjoy friends and conversation.

No photo available

Esther Miller was born in 1912 in a little town in Indiana. She started her career working in a telephone office when she was fifteen years old. Later she married and moved to Benton Harbor with her husband and raised their three children. She worked as a secretary for twenty-five years. Esther assisted her husband, a semi invalid, for many years. She moved to Friendship Village after his death and became involved in many ministries. She made baby blankets, was a volunteer driver for Shepherd Center, supported other women through the grief process, and made bread for friends.

Phil Miller was born on the 10th of May in 1914. He graduated from Western Michigan State Teachers College. Phil was drafted into the Army in 1941. He was captured by the Germans and was held in Stalag Luft I for thirteen months. After the war, Phil married his wife Ethel and they had seven children. The couple bought an insurance agency where Phil worked into his seventies. After  his retirement, Phil continued to live a challenging and productive life. He was a speaker on a radio program called "Issues on Aging." Here he captivated listeners with his accounts of the Civil War and World War II battles.

 Ray Miller was born in Kalamazoo, Michigan in 1920. In 1941 during World War II, he joined the coast guards. After the war he came home with "wander lust." He began traveling to all fifty states working as a fry cook. In 1969 he spent a year backpacking in South America. He was fortunate to see both the Carnival in Rio and Trinidad and travel extensively in Europe and Africa. After taking care of his ailing parents, he bought a farm in Lawrence, Michigan where he now resides. Here he grows hay, boards horses, splits wood, and cultivates his garden. In the future, he envisions himself traveling through Egypt.

Evelyn Moore was born on January 31, 1920. She grew up in a large family on a truck farm during the depression. She was grateful to her father for teaching her the value of money and hard work. Evelyn was married in 1942 and had two children. She saved money while her husband was in the service and they were able to start a business when he returned home. She worked with Ron while raising her family. Her husband had a stroke in 1986 and she became the caregiver. She was also involved in the Senior Center and enjoys activities with family and friends.

Lydia Bennett Nickerson was born in New Carlisle, Indiana in 1898. She received a teaching certificate from Valparaiso State Normal College. She married Guy Nickerson and had two children. Lydia taught school and Guy worked for the Grand Trunk Railroad. The couple traveled throughout the United States, Europe, and Canada. It was while  celebrating their fiftieth anniversary in Vancouver, Canada that Lydia's husband died. Lydia remained in her home in the small community of Climax were she was surrounded by children, grandchildren, and friends.

Connie Pearson was born on April 23, 1926 in Pennsylvania. She came from an Italian immigrant family with 13 children. Growing up in such a large family taught her to be confident, responsible, and productive. Connie was married and had seven children and is now single. She is a proud grandmother who takes pride in seeing the value system that was instilled in her by her parents being passed down through her children to her grandchildren. She attended college and worked at Borgess Hospital for many years until her retirement in 1992. She moved into a senior complex where she enjoyed crocheting and spending time with friends.

Rosadelle Perry was born in Sturgis, Michigan on August 16, 1913. She was a descent of George Soule who came over on the Mayflower. Rosadelle was married in 1933 and has two wonderful children. During World War II, she joined the work force handling defense bonds for government employees. Later she became bank manager at the Employment Security Commission. She held this position until the age of seventy. Rosadelle was a strong, modern woman with traditional val-

ues. As she said, "I've had it all, a wonderful family and a successful career. What more could a woman ask for?"

Marjorie Pierce was born in Bridge-water, Vermont in 1903. She graduated from the University of Vermont in 1925 and the Sorbonne in Paris in 1930. Upon returning home, she taught high school French and math in Boston, Massachusetts until her retirement in 1958. She became the owner of her father's country store in Vermont in 1967 where she continued to work until she was ninety-two years old. She was involved in Amnesty International, The Ladies Aid Society, and the Historical Society. Marjorie also worked on genealogy charts for her friends and neighbors.

Alba "Polly" Pollard was born in Detroit, Michigan in 1914. On completing high school, she joined the Oblate Sisters of Providence and became a teacher. Later she would be the first educator to integrate a Catholic high school in South Carolina and to start schools in both the South and Midwest. In the sixties she became involved in the civil rights movement, marching with Dr. Martin Luther King. Later, she received

degrees from Loyola University and Western Michigan University. She was then employed at Western until her retirement at the age of 70. Later, she became involved in the National Counsel of Catholic Women.

Gertrude Powell was an extraordinary woman whose life spanned over a century. She was born in 1894 in Battle Creek, Michigan. Gertrude graduated from high school and was married in 1934. Her son, daughter-in-law, grandchildren, and great grandchildren were the loves of her life. She worked for a publishing company and later for the Gilmore Corporation. She was honored at one time for being one of the fourteen oldest mothers in Michigan. When asked on her 105th birthday, what she would you have done differently, she replied, "Nothing, just more of it."

Lorita Powell was born in Gingerland Rd. in Nevis in 1929. She remembers as a child, learning to hoe the land, plant fruit and cotton, and walking a mile to and from school barefoot. She was married at twenty-one and had nine children. When Lorita's husband died, she had to work the fields, tend to the animals, cut the wood, and plant the cotton to support her children. She is a survivor and has been through an earthquake and a hurricane. Today, Lorita enjoys her family, gardening, watching television, and listening to Island music. In 1999, she came to the United States for a visit and flew on a jet plane for the first time.

Elizabeth Purchase was born April 19, 1909 in Grand Rapids, Michigan. She received a teaching certificate from Western Michigan University in 1927 and a Master's Degree twenty years later. Elizabeth taught at Edison School for thirty-five years. In 1960 she spent three years in Nigeria trying to break down cultural barriers. As a member of the Presbyterian Church she has been involved in many ministries. Elizabeth was a founding member of the "Bethlehem Group," which supplied low priced bread and meals to people in need. She also wrote the history of the joint diaconate for her church.

Beth Sambo was born in 1930 in Illinois. While still in high school, Beth took music lessons at Kimball Hall in Chicago.
At the age of seventeen she was a piano soloist for the Chicago Symphony Orchestra. Through the years, Beth has taught piano, sang with the "Sweet Adeline's," directed a children's chorus, and played the organ for church. She is married and has five children. Beth is passionate about her relationships with family and friends, music, cooking, gardening, and reading. Currently, she takes tap dancing lessons at the senior center and is involved in many variety shows.

Lillie King Scott was born in Alabama on February 15, 1915. She was one of nine children and even though her mother had to raise them on her own, they were a loving, close family. Lillie married and moved to Michigan in 1946 and had ten children. Although she has experienced the pain of losing two children and her first husband, Lillie continued to have a zest for life due to her deep belief in God. She had traveled to Hawaii, Florida, and Mexico. Lillie lived with her second husband and took care of children in her home. Her family and extended family all called her "Momma."

Jack Streidl was born on December 7, 1918 in a small Michigan town. He attended Western Michigan University where he played football in 1941. He was a heavy weight boxing champion and wrestled for all four years. The day after the bombing of Pearl Harbor, Jack enlisted in the Navy and received his commission at Columbia University. Jack married his college sweetheart in 1942, had eight children and 22 grandchildren. Jack accepted the position as athletic director at Plainwell High School where he worked until retirement. He received numerous awards and had a football field named after him.

Phyllis Streidl was the third child born into her family on October 10, 1920. She graduated from Western Michigan University just as her mother had before her. She married Jack Streidl in 1942, had eight children and eventually 22 grandchildren. Phyllis was a stay at home mom and raised her three grandchildren after the death of her daughter. Religion is an integral part of Phyllis' life. She attends mass, benediction, and Bible studies. Phyllis is an author and has published a book of poetry. She now enjoys spending time with her husband and having family gatherings at their cottage up north.

Richard Tanner was born in Kalamazoo, Michigan in 1920. He attended Western Michigan University. Later he joined the Army and became a physical training instructor during World War II. He married, had three children, and was employed as a mortgage counselor for thirty-nine years. After his retirement and the death of his wife, he decided to "go see the world." His journeys took him to New Zealand where he Parasailed and to France where he bicycled through the Loire Valley. In 1997, he experienced an earthquake in Assisi, Italy. Richard has been involved in Senior Olympics and has earned numerous medals and trophies. He re-married and continues to travel.

Gordon Ten Brink was born April 30, 1916. He fought in World War II and was proud of his contribution. His wife Elaine was born April 9, 1922. They met, fell in love and were married. Gordon was a plastering contractor and Elaine was a secretary in an office equipment company. They adopted two "special needs" children. Although they had to face the early deaths of both their son and daughter, they thanked God for the time they had them in their lives. Gordon and Elaine celebrated their fiftieth wedding anniversary shortly before Gordon passed.

Ralph Turner was born on August 8, 1902. As a child he played the drums for the seventh infantry for the fiftieth anniversary of the Battle of Gettysburg. Although Ralph had Infantile Paralysis when he was a child, he was able to run the hundred yard dash in high school. Ralph worked for many years as the head of the industrial art department at Allen Electric & Equipment Company. He was married to his wife, Verna, for seventy years and had one son and two grandchildren. After the death of his beloved wife, he moved into an assisted living complex in Kalamazoo until his passing.

Robert Van Blarcom was born in Kalamazoo, Michigan in 1913. After one year of college, he was married and later started his family. He received a degree in education and became a teacher in East Detroit. Leaving the teaching profession, he took a job in a lumber yard and reached his goal by becoming the owner of the company. He sold the business when he was in his early eighties, but continued to be involved in other ventures. He was active in the community and was on the school board for eleven years. Robert Van Blarcom died in 1999.

George Vargish was born in 1913 in New York. His father died in 1920 which left his mother the sole supporter of his family. His mother, a proud woman, taught him the importance of hard work. He graduated from New York University and started working in the textile industry. He became a prominent businessman and served as an advisor for our government on bilateral trade, was an author, and speaker. His family included his wife his daughter Nancy, grandchildren, and great grandchildren. He served three terms as Mayor of Saddle River, New Jersey where he presently lives with his wife.

Viola Weber and her twin sister were born on December 13, 1922. She was one of six children who grew up on her parent's farm in the Upper Peninsula. Eventually, Viola left the farm to seek employment and moved to Detroit, Michigan. Later she joined the Air Corps and was part of the air transport command. After leaving the service, she started working for Plymouth Factory and retired from Chrysler thirty-one years latter. Viola learned to love animals on the farm and had a horse all her life. She started showing her first horse Rocky in the early fifties and later showed Wimpy who went on to be a champion. Viola continues to enjoy her horse and teaching others how to care for them.

Hilda Wesseling was born in Sparta, Michigan in 1917. She married Milo Wesseling in 1944 and the couple had two children. While raising her children, she also worked in food services in an elementary school. She retired from her job many years later to take care of her husband who was ill. After his death, she opened an Adult Foster Care home. The residence became part of her extended family. Hilda's life is one of love and service to others. Due to her own health problems, Hilda moved to a senior complex. While there, she continued to care for others by serving Meals on Wheels.

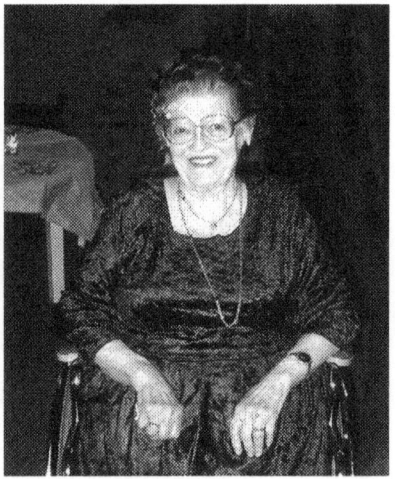

Zheng Geng was born in May of 1929 in China. She grew up on a farm and did not start her education until later in life because her family was very traditional. Zheng graduated from college with a degree in early education. She began her career as a preschool teacher. She was married and had three children. Once her family was started, she worked at the library in a middle school. She overcame illness through exercise and positive thinking. She finds her happiness being around children. She came to America for the first time to see her daughter, son-in-law, and grandchild.

Xiugang Wu was born in China in 1929. He was a farmer, then an elementary teacher, and later worked for the Chinese government until his retirement. Xiugang was married and raised three children. His one son is at the British University, his other son works for the government, and his daughter who has a Master's Degree from China and one from Western Michigan University lives in the United States. Xiugang exercises three to four hours a day and finds his happiness from his wife, children, and grandchildren. After his visit to the United States, he was looking forward to returning home to China.

APPENDIX

▼

FAMILY TREASURE

This book was designed to celebrate
the lives of seniors.
We hope you will use this section
for pictures and
cherished memories
of your loved one.

Place Picture Here

Place Biography Here

What do you believe is your greatest contribution?

What does love mean to you?

What are your thoughts on death and dying?

What lessons has life taught you?

What are your thoughts about the changes you have experienced in your lifetime?

What has been your greatest challenge?

How do you deal with crisis in your life?

What words do you have for the younger generation?

What makes you happy?

Have you ever experienced a miracle in your life?

What do you do to stay healthy?

What is you most vivid memory?

What does spirituality mean in your life?

What do you think makes a successful marriage?

About the Authors

Loretta Martin and **Susan Massoud** are sisters who live in Michigan. Loretta began working with seniors while pursing a post graduate degree. Susan is a special education teacher whose past time is genealogy. Loretta's experience with seniors and Susan's involvement in family history, became the driving force behind the book they co-authored *"Hearts of Seniors."* Working on this endeavor, strengthened the bound between sisters. It also confirmed Loretta's belief that all of mankind is threads woven in the tapestry of life and the threads of these seniors who were interviewed for the book were exceptionally strong and wonderfully colored.

978-0-595-41581-6
0-595-41581-4

www.ingramcontent.com/pod-product-compliance
Lightning Source LLC
Chambersburg PA
CBHW020436290526
45785CB00002B/870